AF291990

The Roots
of Francisco de Goya

J. Carlos Arroyos

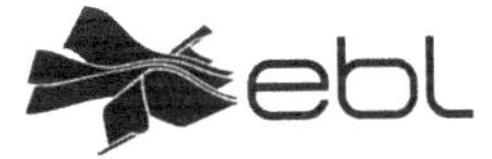

The Roots of Francisco de Goya

English version of *Las raíces de Goya*, revised, updated and with illustrations of Goya's works

First Edition: 2022

ISBN: 9781524318154
ISBN eBook: 9781524328283

© of the text:
  J. Carlos Arroyos

© of the translation:
  Nicola Stapleton

© Layout, design and production of this edition: 2022 EBL

*For my wife Carmen, for her help and patience
while I was writing this book during the long days
of lockdown in 2020-2021 when the Covid-19 pandemic hit.*

*Doing easily what others find difficult is talent;
doing what is impossible for talent is genius.*

HENRI-FRÉDÉRIC AMIEL

Table of Contents

Lists of Illustrations

Introduction

The 30th of March 2021 marks the 275th anniversary of the birth of universal artist and genius Francisco de Goya y Lucientes in the village of Fuendetodos in Aragón.

Interest never fades in his life and work, and many commemorative exhibitions, lectures and cultural events were held throughout the year. The following is a selection:

- King Felipe VI of Spain and Queen Letizia marked the start of the *Year of Goya* with a visit to his birthplace in Fuendetodos. The exhibition of Aragonese artist Fernando Martín Godoy, *The Ghostly Gaze* and *Solana versus Goya. Mask and Simulation* went on show at the Sala Ignacio Zuloaga (Exhibition Hall).
- Fuendetodos has hosted a number of events on Goya and his work, including mural painting and street sculpture, talks at Goya's childhood home, exhibitions at Sala Zuloaga and in the Etchings Museum, and entertainment in the form of dance, film and music. A lyric opera gala took place in the Church of Our Lady of the Assumption featuring soprano Montserrat Martí, mezzo-soprano Beatriz Gimeno, baritone Luis Santana and tenor Alain Damas.
- The Metropolitan Museum of New York presented *Goya's Graphic Imagination*. The exhibition poster featured *Seated Giant,* representing an omnipotent being — war, plague or perhaps the current Covid-19- pandemic — which looks on impassively as the terrified humans it threatens to destroy flee in every direction.
- The anthological exhibition at the Basel Fondation Beyeler commemorated the Argonese painter through *Goya Prophet of Modernism* presenting seventy-five of his paintings, fifty drawings and fifty etchings.

- The National Gallery of Victoria (NGV) in Melbourne presented an exclusive exhibition of more than 160 drawings entitled *Goya: Drawings from the Prado Museum*.

- The exhibition at Palacio de Sástago *El joven Goya y las pinturas de Fuendetodos* (Young Goya and his Fuendetodos paintings) was organized by the provincial government of Zaragoza. It featured a virtual reconstruction of a mural Goya had painted depicting a baldachin over the cupboard where the relics were kept in the parish church of Fuendetodos. This is his first known work.

- The Ibercaja-Camón Aznar collection at the Goya Museum in Zaragoza exhibited *La Estela de Corrado Giaquinto en España: de González Velázquez y Bayeu a Goya*, from 24 June to 26 September 2021. It included seven works by Goya, three of which were recently attributed to him.

- Fundación Ibercaja sponsored ten videoconferences including one by Agustín Sánchez Vidal called *Goya y el cine*, which traced how the universal message of Goya and his art has featured in film from its earliest origins. Another by Ignacio Calvo and Amparo Martínez was entitled *De la imaginación a la imagen. Goya y Buñuel* and a third by Juan Bolea discussed *Enigmas en torno a Goya*.

- Renowned Spanish film director Carlos Saura released his short film *Goya. 3 de mayo* which deals with the madness of war.

- The Pablo Serrano Museum in Zaragoza organized *Poéticas surrealistas. Arte aragonés contemporáneo* which established a dialogue between the works of Goya and those of young contemporary artists. In November the audiovisual show *Goya sin límites* went on display in the auditorium, featuring a 360º projection which immersed the viewer in the dreamlike world of Goya.

- Zaragoza's University Library held the bibliographic exhibition *Goya, historia y crítica,* featuring works in its holdings, and a major collection of specialized work from the María Moliner and General Universitaria libraries.

- The Museum of Huesca launched initiatives and activities related to Goya's work called *Tierra de Goya,* with a selection of the artist's lithogaphs in Room 7, and the Bulls of Bordeaux in Room 8.

- The Bank of Spain, founded by Charles III in 1782 as the San Carlos Bank, presented the origins of its own collection of paintings entitled *R.v.on 2.328* in a reference to the *reales de vellón* coins paid to Goya for painting the bank's director at that time, José Moñino y Redondo, the First Count of Floridablanca.

- The Spanish Association of Painters and Sculptors organized a special exhibition on the 275th anniversary of Goya's birth at Sala Eduardo Úrculo in Madrid, which featured the work of many different artists.

- The Fernán Gómez Theatre in Madrid presented an immersive experience *#INGOYA* where the visitor was plunged into the universe of Goya's work to the accompaniment of classical music.

- The new Helga de Alvear Museum in Cáceres dedicated one of its rooms to Goya in recognition of his great influence on modern and contemporary works of art.

- Fundación Bancaja organized an exhibition on Goya's legacy in Picasso's work, entitled *Goya en la mirada de Picasso. Grabadores* in Valencia. Divided into four areas, *Mirada de Juventud* (The Youthful Gaze*); The Dream of Reason Produces Monsters; La Tauromaquia como fiesta;* and Goya in Picasso's texts.

- Four books were published in Spain over the year about various aspects of Goya's life and work, in addition to *Las raíces de Goya*. They include: *Goya en el país de los garrotazos* by Berna González, *El encargo del maestro Goya* by Elena Bargues, *Martín Zapater, amigo de Goya y noble de Aragón* by Antonio Peiró Arroyo and *El retrato de la madre de Goya* by Domingo J. Buesa. In Germany *Francisco de Goya Träume und Alpträume - Briefe.*

- To bring the celebrations of Goya's 275th birthday to a close, at the end of December, the Goya Museum in Zaragoza organized an exhibition called *Goya, traveller and artist of the Grand Tour,* covering the artist's trip to Italy, his experience in Rome and its significance in his work.

Sadly, the Prado Museum — home to the world's greatest collection of Goya's works — did not organize an extensive exhibition on the richness of his life and pictorial diversity on this occasion, while continuing to misrepresent certain aspects of the character and work of the genius from Aragón.

For its part, *The Roots of Francisco de Goya* aims to acquaint the reader with hitherto little-known aspects of Goya's life during his years in Aragón, from his birth in Fuendetodos in 1746 until he moved to Madrid after he married, in 1775. It seeks to identify experiences from his childhood, adolescence and early youth which nourished the roots from which his spirit and intelligence sprang.

As we shall see in the first four chapters, Goya was born in Fuendetodos where he lived until the age of thirteen. This little village, which at the time had a population of about four hundred, was a simple farming community surrounded by pine forest and rain-fed arable land, punctuated with small vineyards and olive groves, and deep ravines known as *foces* — carved by nature over thousands of years of wind and runoff erosion — and home to diverse flora and fauna. Summers would have been warm and sunny, while snow — frequent in winter — was kept in covered pits, where it became ice that was then transported on carts overnight to the city of Zaragoza where it was sold.

The village school in Fuendetodos had one section for boys and another for girls. Pupils would have taken part in many activities and events all year round, particularly festivals and celebrations, drawing on the customs and practices that would have been traditional in a village at that time, and which would have been influenced by its recent incorporation into the territories of the Crown of Aragon.

Now, activities, events and exhibitions celebrating Goya's life and work take place in Fuendetodos throughout the year, allowing thousands of visitors to discover the place where the artist grew up.

Subsequent chapters deal with Goya's arrival in Zaragoza, where he studied for two years at the Piarists' School and began his professional training as an apprentice at the art academy of the painter José Luzán. It was during this time that Goya became friends with fellow students Martín Zapater and the Bayeu brothers, as well as Martín Goicoechea.

Zaragoza was a modern city for the time and the former capital of the Kingdom of Aragón from which it had inherited its economic, social and political legacy. Here, Goya took an active part in its culture and entertainment, including literary, musical and courtship gatherings or salons held in high-society homes. He attended theatre performances at the Casa de Comedias playhouse, enjoyed *romerías* — where pilgrims walked and socialized together in honour of religious figures — and shared in lively communal picnics in the countryside with other young people. He was a great fan of bullfights, which were followed by rowdy nights of singing, dancing, and drinking that went on in the local taverns into the early hours of the morning. Fiery and rambunctious, he got involved in popular uprisings like Broqueleros — Zaragoza's equivalent of the Esquilache Riots in Madrid — caused by the hunger and terrible living conditions which blighted the city.

From late 1770 to June 1771, he travelled to Italy at his own expense, where he became acquainted with classical works that he would later incorporate into his own repertoire. In Rome, he associated with high-ranking political representatives of Spain some of whom, like him, were from Aragón. On their advice, he submitted an entry to Parma's major painting competition on the theme of Hannibal's arrival in Italy and won second prize.

During his years in Zaragoza, Goya's output was prolific, with work dedicated particularly to religious subjects. After marrying Josefa, sister of his friends, the Bayeu brothers, he moved to Madrid at the age of twenty-nine to work as cartoon painter at the Royal Tapestry Factory run by German artist Raphael Mengs.

In his tapestry cartoons, Goya emerged as an artist both of and for the people. Considered the first Spanish Romantic painter, he depicted both the magic of nature and the diverse customs of common folk, with their faults and their virtues. In his portraits — of which there are more than four hundred — he was able to capture the spirit of the sitter, whether monarch, aristocrat, bullfighter, performing artist, entrepreneur or just a friend: he portrayed people at every social level. After arriving in Madrid, he experienced turbulent times marked by war, revolution and authoritarian governments, the malign effects of which are featured in his work. His enlightened, liberal outlook ultimately forced him into exile in Bordeaux, where he died in 1828.

I would like to express my gratitude to Professor María Antonia Martín Zorraquino, the widow of my good and dearly missed friend, Professor Juan Rivero Lamas, who has helped this book see the light of day. She was able to appreciate my burning desire to provide a proper record of Goya's origins in Aragón, which I have studied passionately and meticulously over many years and which, in my view, have never been sufficiently taken into account in the literature which analyse his incomparable artistic prowess.

I would also like to express my gratitude to Nicola Stapleton for her splendid translation from the original Spanish text.

Chapter 1

I Saw It

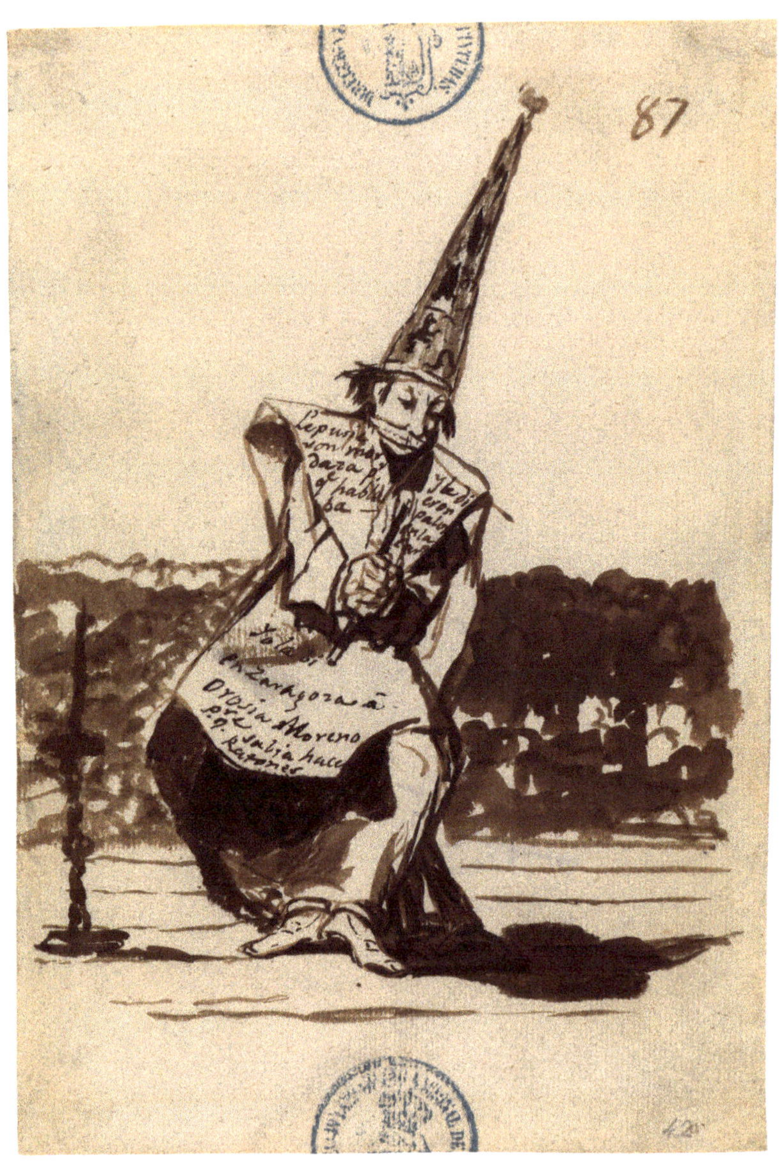

I saw her, Orosia Moreno, in Zaragoza.
Punished because she knew how to make mice.
© Prado Museum Photographic Archive

There are many biographies of Francisco de Goya y Lucientes which express unjustified and inconsistent opinions about the early years of the artist's life. Some of his first French biographers made the mistake — unwittingly and perhaps because accurate information was not available to them — of depicting him as a novelesque and sometimes violent adventurer. Other Spanish authors have associated Goya's strong and irritable character with the events he experienced in a time of upheaval and with the emergence of revolutionary ideas.

Most of the best-known biographies focus on Goya's period in Madrid, neglecting his life as a child and teenager in Aragón and have particularly misconstrued the time he spent in Fuendetodos, the village where he was born. I have referred to biographies of his childhood and youth, as well as research on the Aragonese and rural society of his day in an attempt to consider his development as an individual and his sense of self, and how this spurred him into becoming the great artist we know today.

My aim is to make pertinent connections and shed light on important, but hidden or little-known aspects of Goya's upbringing in Aragón and how they lived on in the great master and his work throughout his life. We will consider that sense of self which the Spanish philosopher Ortega y Gasset (1962) refers to as flying "above a future which moves ahead of everything that already is, and which is consequently ahead of our present, from which we are constantly lunging towards the not-here-yet." We will consider Goya's life in Fuendetodos and Zaragoza and elaborate on his oeuvre from that time with particular emphasis on the influence of the personal experiences he accumulated before he left Aragón and moved to Madrid in 1775.

One of Goya's defining characteristics is continuity. Although he never stopped learning and incorporating everything new with which he became acquainted over the course of his life — be they life events or the emergence and use of new techniques — he never forgot his past experiences. As expressed in one of the famous prints etched in old age: ***I am still learning***, he always stayed up to date, adopting different painting styles throughout his life, including Baroque, Neoclassical and Romantic, and kept up with developments in techniques ranging from fresco to aquatint, lithography and painting on all kinds of media, even in miniature.

In his work, this continuity takes the form of ideas, landscapes, people, and things discovered in his childhood and youth in Aragón, in the permanent mental presence of his Aragonese family and in his care and dedication to friends like Martín Zapater, whom he met at the age of thirteen at the Piarists' School and with whom he frequently corresponded over a period of 23 years.

Goya never forgot where he came from, but — perhaps affected by condescending attitudes to rural society — he confines his epistolary recollections to the years after his arrival in Zaragoza to study with the Piarists and appears to draw a veil over his life in Fuendetodos. Consequently, the letters Goya wrote to his friend and schoolmate Martín Zapater deal only with their shared experiences in Zaragoza and are sadly the only major source of correspondence known today. Therefore, we are unable to complete our picture of his life in Fuendetodos with the content of other letters he may have written to his mother, relatives or friends.

Goya's choice of expression and vocabulary in his letters to Zapater is always simple and direct, sometimes to the point of vulgarity. Indeed, some authors have misinterpreted these letters as a sign that Goya was a rough, uncouth yokel, going so far as to claim he was devoid of any book learning and even that he wrote badly. His choice of words is more likely a deliberate desire to revert to the expressions of the youth and adolescence that Goya and Zapater had shared, in a bid to relive those early days of their friendship all the more intensely. By continuing this tone of voice in his letters to Zapater, Goya may also have wished to record and illustrate the vast artistic and cultural distance that separated his early years in Fuendetodos and Zaragoza from his subsequent success in Madrid. Indeed, at the same time he was using such loutish, easy-going, humorous language with Zapater, he was also writing stylish, erudite letters in the form of artistic recommendations. The following letter sent to the San Fernando Royal Academy of Fine Arts in Madrid in 1792 refers to the study of the arts in general and of painting in particular:

> I consider there to be no rules in painting and that oppression, or a servile obligation to make everybody study or follow the same path, is a very great impediment for young people who practise an art as difficult as this which, more than any other, touches the Divine, by representing everything that God has created.

He concludes with the following words:

> What profound and impenetrable mystery is enclosed within the emulation of Divine Nature, such that, without it, there can be nothing good, not only in painting (which seeks no other purpose than its immediate imitation), but also in the other sciences!

The depth with which a child's feelings are carved into the psyche is universal. Those early recollections are fixed, stored, and retrieved, as described in this extract by Mexican agronomist Luciano Pool Novelo (2015):[1]

> I am from Holpechén, Campeche. I left my village when I was twenty and returned to the state some 27years later. What I remember from my childhood is that I was always free: in the orchards, eating fruit from the trees, shooting birds with a catapult, playing marbles with friends, and going into the forest to cut firewood; sometimes my father would take me to the cornfields to bring back the maize he was harvesting. In November, on the Day of the Dead, we would leave in the early morning mist. I have one clear memory of the burning season in April, at Easter, when the sun would go deep red, and you could look straight at it.

In a similar vein, the distinguished cartoonist, illustrator and writer Antonio Mingote, a member of Spain's Royal Academy of Language also from Aragón, said (2008):

> A man's true story is the story of his childhood and teenage years: that's my story. That's simply where I am: in Aragón, in Teruel, in Daroca, in Zaragoza, in Calatayud. All my biography is there, even though the place I've lived longest is Madrid. But adolescence and childhood have plenty to say when it comes to one's biography.

It is in infancy, childhood, and early adolescence when a person's psyche undergoes its developmental stages, and

---

[1] Luciano Pool Novelo is an agricultural engineer who specializes in soil at the Universidad Autónoma Chapingo. He is Master of Sciences in Edaphology and an agricultural expert at Ecosur.

intelligence forms.[2] The Swiss psychologist Jean Piaget (1966) defined the following four stages in this development:

- The sensorimotor stage, from birth to age two develops through signalling systems from subjects and objects on the one hand, and words on the other. The child adapts to his or her environment and sensorial learning gradually gives way to mastery of language.

- The preoperational stage, aged two to seven, represents a transition from practical to representational intelligence and objects that are not directly perceptible can be symbolized, such as images in books, films, and videos, or in spatially distributed shapes in diverse colours. In this phase, first-hand knowledge and direct observation of nature are crucial. The child asks many questions in a bid to broaden his or her knowledge of the real world around them.

- Logic and mathematical structures develop at the age of seven to eleven, when the child uses logic to resolve the problems posed by concrete objects and events. The instrument used is intuitive reasoning which leads them to generalize through observation, deductive reasoning. Children understand perspectives other than their own. Abstract thought begins and they consider the outcome of their actions. They are able to feel love and understand logical values which allow them to glimpse future possibilities and gauge what they are able to achieve. They begin to develop adolescent egocentricity with attention-seeking behaviour and try to show their supreme uniqueness.

---

[2] This reference to the developmental stages in individual psychology draws on J. Piaget (1966), and the notes of Luis Roger Quant, Doctor in Law from Universidad Nacional Autónoma de Nicaragua.

- With formal operations, at the age of eleven to fifteen, they are able to develop deductive hypothetical reasoning which allows them to predict the results and consequences of a specific event from general principles. They resolve problems with logic and reassert their individuality. Their egocentricity is accentuated, and abstract thought develops.

It was during these four stages of Goya's life, when many of the images which Goya would recall many years later were etched upon his mind. The male goat depicted in **Witches' Sabbath** (*El Aquelarre*) is a case in point, reminiscent of the bucks which, with their greater size, strength, and swagger, would have dominated the flocks of sheep that grazed in his grandfather's meadows in Fuendetodos. Nor did Goya forget the brutality of bandits and highwaymen that he would later paint in many memorable pictures.

Diverse types of farm work are also recalled in the series of tapestry cartoons **Spring, Summer, Autumn, Winter** (*Primavera, verano, otoño, invierno)*, as are the hunts in which Goya took part, depicted in paintings like **Hunter Loading His Rifle** (*El cazador cargando su escopeta)*. Countryside pilgrimages, known as *romerías*, and other events which he took part in or witnessed in his early years also feature prominently in his work.

According to Benjamín Jarnés (1988), "although Madrid may have been Goya's main workshop, before the workshop where the painting is created, we must consider the workshop which created the painter." In this respect, Goya's biographers express very different opinions about how he was "discovered" as a painter. In an account provided by August L. Mayer (1925), it was the Count of Fuentes and Lord of Fuendetodos who came across the young Goya painting a fresco on the wall behind a reliquary in the parish church. It was to accompany the oil paintings he had himself painted on the doors, known as ***Coming of Our Lady of the Pillar to Zaragoza*** (*Venida de la Virgen del Pilar a Zaragoza*). Surprised by his artistic skill, the Count is said to have taken charge of the young artist's education.

Despite the alternative hypothesis that the young Goya had by this stage moved to Zaragoza with his parents for good, it is not impossible that he could have painted the work when returning on holiday. The anecdote also alludes to the undoubted friendship between the Count of Fuentes and Goya's family, which the painter continued to cultivate for the rest of his life.

In other accounts, it has been noted that the priest of Fuendetodos was one of the first to recognize young Francisco's precocious talent for drawing and that he allowed the boy to help paint the parish church, probably during one of his summer holidays in the village. His work on the paintings in the sacristy reliquary dates from 1762 or 1763, when Goya would have been sixteen or seventeen; but that work, like the other parish church paintings, was burned and destroyed during the Spanish Civil War in 1936; local residents who witnessed the devastation claimed that the cabinet doors had been removed before the fire, but their whereabouts is unknown.

Baticle (2004) refers to the same story, claiming it may have been the priest to whom legend attributes the discovery of Goya's skill when he drew on the walls of barns as a boy.

But the clergyman in question could also have been Vicente Pignatelli, brother of the Count of Fuentes, who was responsible for the Archdiocese of Belchite, 20 kilometres from Fuendetodos.

José Baeza (1928) refers to an old friar and friend of Luzán, who discovered him drawing the perfect figure of a pig on the white wall of a mill in Fuendetodos, using a piece of charcoal he had found on the ground. He claims the friar spoke to Goya's father and convinced him to go and work in Luzán's workshop, where his work would be remunerated, if not lavishly, at least with enough to live on. But this account may have drawn on Vasari's biography (1568) of Giotto.

Wirth reference to a similar story to that of Giotto, Onieva (1973) describes the child artist drawing with charcoal on a whitewashed wall when he was discovered by a friar, who may have been the Prior of the Charterhouse of Aula Dei, Father Félix Salcedo, who spotted Goya's great talent for drawing and spoke to his father. This led to the decision to send him both to the Piarist school in Zaragoza and to study drawing at José Luzán's academy. This version may be closer to the truth, as the Carthusians of Aula Dei were indeed clients of Goya's grandfather, Miguel, who supplied ice from his Culroya icehouse for the storage of medicines and perishable foods. Years later, Goya painted the cycle of frescoes on the **Life of the Virgin** *(La vida de la Virgen)* on the walls of the Carthusian church.

According to his friend Zapater, Goya commented on these paintings when he returned to Fuendetodos in 1808 during the Peninsular War. On visiting the village church, he claimed not to believe he had painted the reliquary pictures and warned his friends against "telling anyone that I painted that!" Perhaps he was unwilling to acknowledge that the work — necessarily naïve and unskilled — could have been produced by his own hand. Only one previous work of his is known: a copy of Cortona's **Tobias and the Archangel** *(Tobías y el arcángel)*, also painted in 1762, probably during his apprenticeship at Luzán's academy.

Information obtained directly from Fuendetodos residents acquainted with Goya suggest he was almost certainly a mischievous and restless boy who scribbled figures on the walls of village farm buildings. His attachment to the countryside became ingrained in him from infancy and childhood in his native Fuendetodos where he would have produced these first

simple drawings of the rural world: a horse, a goat, a hare, a tree...
But the decisive factor in his becoming a painter was probably
the artistic appreciation of his grammar teacher in Zaragoza,
the Jesuit José de Pignatelli — another brother of the Count of
Fuentes — who noticed the excellent technique of the pictures
Goya drew in the margins of his books in class-time and advised
his father that he should work as a painter. Once he finished
school, his father signed him up as an apprentice with Luzán, on
a recommendation from the Baroque painter's brother, whom he
had assisted in a lawsuit.

The teaching of grammar was the exclusive preserve of the
Jesuits, and it was a subject Goya learned at the Piarists' school,
where he met Father Pignatelli. He later visited him in Naples,
on his trip to Italy, where Pignatelli went to live after the Jesuit
expulsion from Spain in 1767. José de Pignatelli became the
provincial superior of the Jesuits in Italy under the protection
of the non-Catholic Catherine the Great of Russia. This would
also explain why the Russian ambassador to Italy, a friend of
both Pignatelli and the Spanish ambassador to Italy — Nicolás
de Azara, also from Aragón — was acquainted with Goya's work
and offered him work at the empress's court. Goya declined,
believing that his family needed him in Zaragoza.

Thus, it was that a country boy from a modest background in
a small village in Aragón, began his career as a painter who would
achieve fame as an artist, first in Zaragoza and later in Madrid,
where he came to frequent the palaces of the court and Madrid's
nobility, and paint portraits at the highest echelons of Spanish
society: a painter who would become known as a universal genius. Goya's son Javier wrote that his father's works "are evidence
that nothing in painting remained for him to overcome and he
discovered magic, a word which he always used to express the
ambiance of a picture." That magic arose from the observation

of his first teacher, nature. It helps to explain why he was against rules, affectation, and academicism, instead advocating the free exercise of genius and understanding in the depiction of a landscape, an atmosphere or the spirit of the people represented in his paintings.

Another element of Goya's magic is colour. As well as rejecting lines, he claimed that colour did not exist, that there was only light and shade, and that the secret of painting resided in proper study of the object, and in resolute execution, because "black and white suffice to make pictures."

Goya painted a vast number of works which, over the space of 250 years, have generated an avalanche of books and articles on his life and output, his personality, and his relationship to the history of his day. His paintings are coveted by art galleries and private collections all over the world. The largest and most representative collection is housed in the Prado Museum in Madrid and include the murals, or **Black Paintings**, from the walls of his villa, known as Quinta del Sordo, by the river Manzanares where the enigmatic and paradigmatic **Dog** has pride of place.

Goya's skill, emphasized by many authors, at reflecting the intangible and idealizing the tangible, is referred to by the Count of La Viñaza (1887) as "*mens divinior*", that rare virtue that has accompanied martyrs, heroes, sages, and artists to the temple of immortality. The artist himself described it thus "I recognize and wish for no teacher beside nature, Rembrandt and Velázquez." And the first of these three masters to which Goya paid tribute is his most important: it was in his childhood and birthplace that he discovered, experienced, and breathed nature, and, with his genius, made it his for ever. It is from that first contact with nature that his pictures of children were born, drawn from the memories he later recalled of his siblings playing in Fuendetodos, climbing trees in the orchard opposite his house or running in and out of the castle walls. But nature, in all its facets, must be "seen"; it is not enough simply to look; artists have to be able to distinguish and interpret the content in what they observe.

Goya's life and work have been analysed and discussed in a wealth of biographies, academic studies, and articles of every kind. But so far, no publication has focused on the purely personal aspect and the influence on the great master's paintings of his immense love for nature, as experienced in the rural Spain of his day, which provides the background for virtually all his work, with the exception of portraits painted in interiors.

In his 1792 report to the San Fernando Royal Academy of Fine Arts, he writes:

> What statue or shape of one has not been copied from Divine Nature, however excellent the master who copied it. When one is placed beside the other, how can I cease to exclaim that one is the work of God while the other is that of our own miserable hands?

Magic for Goya was the capacity of genius to move away from rules and reflect nature. He was no "urbanite", as we might say today, but a man of the country. Indeed, towards the end of his life in1819, he bought and moved to a small farm on the outskirts of Madrid, known as Quinta del Sordo (Villa of the Deaf Man), with nine and a half hectares of arable land, on which he planted all kinds of vegetable.

His passion for hunting was also rural in origin. In one letter to his friend Martín Zapater, he appears to take more pride in his shooting accomplishments in the company of the Marquis of Peñafiel than in his recent paintings. His knowledge of game, acquired on his days out in the Fuendetodos countryside, enhanced his depiction of a freshly killed animal — still in death throes after an accurate shot — in the series of still lifes painted between 1806 and 1812, including ***Still Life with Dead Hares*** *(Liebres muertas)*. Other still lifes with dead and skinned animals, their flesh still smooth but limp, are also a precursor of the prints showing human death in ***The Disasters of War*** *(Los Desastres de la Guerra)*, where the corpses are piled high.

One of the oldest pictures attributed to Goya shows the Fuendetodos landscape. It is a small oil painting of a village woman walking along a country road holding her daughter's hand. Trees are painted to the left of the landscape and the composition of the blue sky is particularly striking, with light cloud and shades of red and mauve which contrast harmoniously with the rest of the picture. A building emerges from a hill to the right. This simple, powerful landscape may well have been the point of departure for some of Goya's later paintings. Particularly significant in this respect is ***The Flower Girls or Spring*** *(Las floreras o La primavera)*, the main theme of which is once again a woman holding her daughter's hand. To the left is a tree and on the right a hill with a building. The atmosphere created by the sky and clouds in blue, white and red retain the same charm as the original picture.

Hunting Party *(Partida de caza)* adopts the same layout. The hunters in the centre are drawn on two different planes with their dogs and animals; on the left are the trees, and on the right buildings on a hill. Above, the sky has light cloud in beautifully contrasting shades of pink and blue. This arrangement with the main characters in the middle, surrounded by a striking landscape with trees, a building on a hill in the background and a colourful sky often recurs in Goya's work. The magnificent ***Picnic on the banks of the Manzanares*** *(La merienda a orillas del Manzanares)* is a case in point. Used for the series of tapestries intended for the dining room at the Royal Palace of El Pardo, its central theme is taken from a farcical sketch by dramatist Ramón de la Cruz.

The countryside, landscapes and rural customs depicted by Goya are always Spanish. Only in his portrait the ***Marquesa of Pontejos*** is the background more British, in the style of the English paintings of the day, at the request, according to some authors, of the sitter herself. He injected plenty of spirit into what the Duke and Duchess of Osuna called "country matters" when these were the main feature of his pictures.

In this regard, ***The Four Seasons*** — the series of tapestry cartoons commissioned by the Osunas for their El Pardo dining room — are particularly outstanding. Painted between 1786 and 1787, they can now be admired in the Prado Museum in Madrid. Here Goya is no mere photographer of nature, but copies it from memory, interpreting and lending it character in the process, according to the customs and precepts of the day among great Spanish painters of the seventeenth and eighteenth century. Of the four cartoons, the picture which perhaps best represents country life, for its realism and spontaneity is ***The Threshing Ground or Summer*** (*La era* or *El Verano*). Goya paints the countryside without actually showing it. This is clearly the summer cereal harvest, but he paints the ears of corn rather than the cornfield and, in three pyramid shapes, depicts the castle, the wheat sheaves and a group of people, scenes he would often have witnessed in his years in Fuendetodos. In this allegory, the artist reflects not the exertions of harvesting, but the simplicity of a welcome break for the peasant farmers. Three young men are trying to get the village idiot drunk, while two children play with the father. A mother is feeding her young son. A man is taking a nap. Three children are playing on top of the grain piled high on the cart. The one at the top, brandishing a two-pronged pitchfork while his mother tries to warn him he might fall off, may well be the first of the twenty-four self-portraits painted by Goya. Perhaps he was remembering a scene he had so often experienced as a child. Ortega y Gasset (1962) highlights "the strange distance of his character, perhaps the artist himself, from the main theme." Goya paints himself as a unique observer, up high, distant, and dominant, with an easy and relaxed smile and expression. At school all year round, unlike the other lads in the picture, Goya might indeed have felt superior. He was also a regular visitor to Aragón's capital Zaragoza, where his father worked. As on other occasions, such as ***La Tauromaquia or Bullfighting*** series, the figures of the people are out of proportion with the horses. Perhaps he wished to introduce this memory at a later stage or deliberately chose to emphasize the size of the animals as they would have appeared to him as a child, distorting the perspective.

Jeannine Baticle (2004) states that the views of Fuendetodos "look as if they have come out of one of Goya's tapestry cartoons: a wild and splendid region that is scorching hot in summer and freezing in winter, where the effects of the light can magically transform landscapes, depending on the time, the day or the season." Nature had to be painted, not copied, to give it its sublime character in line with the precepts Goya followed, but which, with his genius for invention, he took further still to what has been called "the terrible sublime", where he introduces dramatic, surprising, and harsh effects in the midst of nature, as in ***Assault of Thieves*** (*Asalto de ladrones*) of 1794. It depicts a scene of violent death, but in a landscape that is undoubtedly one of the dry, rocky and lonely roads of rural Aragón; the same is true of the oil painting ***The Manufacture of Gunpowder in Sierra de Tardienta*** (*Fabricación de pólvora y balas en los arbolados montes de Tardienta*), during the Peninsular War. With reference to this war, one of Goya's biographers, Hugh

Thomas (1979) suggests the direct relevance of the landscape to the painter's life, where the hillock which forms the backdrop to the shootings is less the colour of Madrid and more like the isolated lunar landscape around Fuendetodos. He also refers to the prominent site of the monastery or church in the background, a reflection of the frequent presence, in many Spanish villages including Fuendetodos, of a towering church that ruled over the lives of their inhabitants, both physically and spiritually.

Goya criticised academicians for the way they taught their young apprentice painters:

> Unlike nature, these candid teachers see details in the ensemble and their details are almost always false and conventional. They could spare their young disciples the trouble of spending two years tracing almond-shaped eyes, arch- or heart-shaped mouths, noses like upside-down sevens and oval heads if they simply showed them nature, which is the only true drawing master.

A Romantic painter, who cherished his freedom to create and treated rules with scorn, Goya has also been referred to as a philosopher-artist who expresses human and popular emotion in his print series. From the work of his avowed teacher Rembrandt, Goya learned the importance of handling light and his bright impasto technique. He highlighted the personality, depth, and atmosphere of his portraits with shadows and a play on light and half-light. Goya paid particular attention to Rembrandt's drawings and prints, adopting the etching process in which he became a great master, but also to his paintings, as in the example of ***The Taking of Christ*** (*El prendimiento de Jesús*).

Goya used sketching in the same way that Rembrandt introduced the technique of loose brushwork with thick impasto which was dubbed "rough manner", removed from the prevailing artistic tradition of his day. Both painters use dark tones, and shadows and light to highlight the figures in their work. Like Rembrandt, Goya introduces movement into his figures: their bodies are active while their posture and expression reflect their personal attitudes. Both were prolific etchers and Goya followed specific examples of Rembrandt's execution, like *Self-portrait Frowning* (*Con el ceño fruncido*) from 1630, with tousled hair and stubble on his chin, looking straight at us, reminiscent of the **Self-portrait** painted by Goya in 1796, also expressionistic in style.

Velázquez was Goya's third master. From him, Goya learned the mastery of light and air, key features in so many of his pictures, and used to create what Goya himself described as "the magic of the atmosphere." Velázquez was an expert in background perspective and filling empty space. In his painting of the sky, the light both reaches up into infinity and is concentrated in swift, subtle brushstrokes in the outfits worn by his sitters, a technique used by Goya in his decoration of the King's dress coat in the portrait of **The Family of Charles IV** (*La familia de Carlos IV*).

Goya follows Velázquez's powerful spatial presentation of his figures. He draws on Velázquez's technique in his court personages, placing them face on, sometimes looking straight at the observer, and always interacting directly with them. **The Family of the Infante, Don Luis** (*La familia del Infante don Luis de Borbón*) is a case in point where, like Velázquez in *Las Meninas*, paints himself into the picture, in the foreground beside the viewer, creating a magical three-dimensional scene featuring figures, artist and beholder.

Another sign of Goya's admiration for Velázquez can be found in the cartoons painted for the Royal Tapestry Factory. Here, the diverse treatment of the light, its brilliant intensity, wide range of hues and shades even led to protests by the weavers, owing to the technical difficulty of the work involved in pictures like ***The Pottery Vendor*** (*El cacharrero*) or ***Dance on the Banks of the Manzanares*** (*El baile a orillas del Manzanares*).

Some of his attempts to imitate Velázquez were at first less successful. In his early equestrian portraits, Goya's horses lack the elegance and verve of the painter from Seville, but he would later excel at the art, using foreshortening to endow the animal with an incredible sense of movement. José Manuel Matilla (2019), one of the curators of the Goya print and drawing exhibition at the Prado in 2020 states that "Goya the portrait artist can only be understood from what he learned from Velázquez." It is true that Goya always acknowledged Velázquez as one of his masters, but to assert that his work "can only be understood" in that light is perhaps to go a little too far. We cannot assume that Goya's great portraits could not have existed without Velázquez. Goya's painting is eternal in its own right. He certainly learned from Velázquez's mastery of the portrait, copying his blue Madrid skies and beautifully intricate colour combinations, like those reflected in the cheeks of ***Juan Bautista de Muguiro***. We could of course trace the origins of Goya's pictures much further back, to timeless origins like the cave drawings in Altamira, and to Ancient Greece and Rome. Goya covered Baroque and Neoclassical styles before erupting into Romanticism, Expressionism, and even touching on the Orient in works like ***The Parasol***. Indeed, his portraits are so diverse, they can in themselves be considered the roots for many artistic styles, including Impressionism, abstraction and the continually evolving trends of modern art.

Goya's pictures adopt Velázquez's use of colour, Madrid's bright blue skies and the assured, emphatic depiction of the earlier painter's characters. But the artist from Aragón abandons perfectionist academicism and linearity, opting instead to evoke the life and movement of his sitters. Unlike Velázquez, he delves deeper into the psyche, beyond outward appearance.

Goya painted more than four hundred portraits. He sought to depict reality, reflecting the vice or virtue that characterized his figures: their industriousness or indolence, their arrogance, vanity or simplicity, their goodness, or bad intentions. He evoked repulsiveness in his portrait of ***Ferdinand VII in court dress;*** he depicted unattractiveness in the queen's prying stare in his portrait of ***The Family of Charles IV;*** he could allude to intelligence or lack of discernment, nobility, or coarseness, putting a malicious glint in the eye of ***Juan Antonio Llorente,*** or presenting a mischievous, serene, or steadfast gaze.

He painted what he saw in his sitters, without artifice. He was utterly meticulous, paying as much attention to bodily posture as gaze, the position of their hands or the arrangement of the objects they hold in perfectly formed fingers. Clothes are sumptuous and magnificent in his depiction of royalty, aristocracy, and the upper bourgeoisie, but simple for the clergy. The ***Majas on a Balcony*** are coquettish and provocatively elegant, while common people wear modest attire.

His painting adapted to diverse styles, with loose, sketchy brushwork with its own strength, or dark colours like black, ochre and earth shades to set the scene for his sombre Black Paintings. Goya had the ability to discern and engage with the emotions of others and transfer them on to the canvas, either through facial expression or by careful definition of bodily posture. This he combined with prior knowledge of his sitters, in addition to observation and identification of the traits of those he painted. The melancholy Countess of Chinchón, the haughty Duchess of Alba, the spoilt but good-natured Charles IV, the hardened Duke of Wellington or the mischievous *majas* are all cases in point.

With his natural empathy, Goya got along with monarchs, aristocrats, politicians of different ideologies, bullfighters, actresses and common people. He was acquainted with the personal background of his models, their faults, and their qualities, and learned more about them during the long hours they posed for him, through conversations which gave him a clearer insight into the mindsets of his models, whose character and spirit he then masterfully reflected.

It was perhaps with women that Goya, a fine connoisseur of feminine psychology, best connected. He was able to sensitively portray, not only women's bodily shapes, but the spirit within, the inner strength that defined them. In Goya's portrait, ***Isabel Cobos de Porcel*** is dazzling and self-assured; her face is beautiful with large features and lively, light-coloured eyes. The artist's white brushstrokes add subtle detail to her iris and pupil. Her compelling shape stands out against the black backdrop of her elegant mantilla shawl. In one portrait of his wife, ***Josefa Bayeu*** is more than fifty years of age. Demurely dressed and with little physical charm, she shows her age and looks tired, but is portrayed with infinite fondness and affection.

Goya takes special care in his choice of the diverse colours used in gowns, faces, arms, hands and artistic or rural backgrounds. He meticulously selects the pets or work tools that accompany sitters like the naturalist ***Félix de Azara.***

He presents military men with a look of triumph or resilience. In the equestrian portrait, the ***Duke of Wellington*** is holding the reins with his left hand and a hat in his right, while the portrait of ***Don Pantaleón Pérez de Nenin*** depicts a rather unrefined middling hero with long sideburns, dressed in hussar uniform, his left hand leaning on a huge sabre depicted as if rooted to the ground.

Velázquez offers us the perfection of academicism, but in a colder, more linear style where the characters lack the living force bestowed by Goya. This difference between the extraordinary talent of Velázquez and the genius of Goya brings to mind what the Swiss writer and philosopher Henri-Frédéric Amiel (1856) defined in generic terms: "Doing easily what others find difficult is talent; doing what is impossible for talent is genius."

Engraved into the subconscious of this genius, is Goya's childhood in Fuendetodos where, as in any small village, it is direct observation of the world around you that has the greatest influence: your family, your neighbours, the passing of the seasons, rural society, hunting, festivals, nature... Goya sees with greater depth and sensitivity than other artists. He goes beyond the masterly depiction of the character or action to an intelligent and superior interpretation of what he sees: an endeavour of which not everyone — however clever or enlightened — is capable.

In the protagonists of his drawings, in addition to their physical appearance or the situation in which they are immersed, Goya sees avarice, affection, ignorance, lechery, wickedness, kindliness, terror, violence... in short, the virtues and vices of humanity. This capacity to analyse and discover what lies beneath was something Goya constantly put into practice and is reflected in his work. Goya showed an extraordinary ability to reveal, attest and critique of which not everyone is capable. The following works are testimony to that skill and reflect the significance of eyewitness accounts ("I saw it") in Goya's work:

Even thus he cannot make her out *(Ni así la distingue):* Like the other *Caprichos,* this work is based on real-life experience. A young fop — monocle in hand — closes in on a young prostitute whom he is examining scrupulously. He does not recognise her for what she is and Goya's comment indicates that, to get to know her, an eyeglass is not enough, what is needed is discernment and worldly experience, something this sorry gentleman lacks.

He is learning to see *(Aprende a ver):* A Moor in a turban is looking skywards without using the eyeglass he is holding in his left hand. Unlike the young man in the previous Capricho, here the protagonist has no need of his telescope to interpret the stars in the firmament.

Look at what they cannot see *(Mirar lo que no ven:* This depicts the Cosmorama fairground attraction. A group of men and women, some on their knees, are crowding around a magic box from which a head emerges and looking through spyholes on the sides. Goya comments on how all of them, blind to the trickery, are eagerly looking for the illusion and entertainment based on charlatanism. Reality is distorted by deceit, which prevents them from seeing things as they are.

I saw it in Paris. *(Yo lo he visto en París:* What Goya saw in this case is an old woman, totally covered up, sitting on a simple wooden cart drawn by a dog.

Death of the Mayor of Torrejón on the Stone Seats in the Bullring at Madrid *(Desgracias acaecidas en el tendido de la plaza de Madrid y muerte del alcalde de Torrejón):* Goya adds this comment to his etching: "The bull leapt up at the row of spectators and killed two of them. I saw it." But Goya notes not only the panic of the people close to the bull which has jumped the fence, but also the bloodthirsty attitude of the audience and their satisfaction that those being gored by the bull are precisely those occupying the best seats in the ring, like the Mayor of Torrejón, a village on the outskirts of Madrid. One spectator in the background, observing these events from a safe distance, may represent the people or even the painter himself.

You'll see later *(Después lo verás):* Goya comments on an event that occurred in Aragón, "when I was a boy." The theme is a clergyman who was run over and, in Goya's words, was "very battered by the horse and donkey."

Because she knew how to make mice *(Porque sabía hacer ratones):* In March 1814, Ferdinand VII restored the Inquisition in Spain, and in this drawing, a seated woman accused of witchcraft has been bound and gagged and is wearing a dunce's cap in a scene surrounded by people. In the full title, Goya states: "since she went on talking, they muzzled her and beat her in the face. I saw her, Orosia Moreno, in Zaragoza. Punished because she knew how to make mice."

I am still learning *(Aún aprendo):* Even in his eighties, when he was living in Bordeaux, Goya still kept his artist's eye wide open, as depicted in this drawing of a bent and bearded old man moving forwards surefootedly with the help of his two walking sticks, his penetrating gaze meeting that of the observer. This is Goya's final self-portrait, dressed in the coarse sackcloth of the Franciscan friars and emulating the features and beard used in other pictures to depict their patron, Saint Francis of Paola, the habit in which Goya asked to be buried.

I saw it *(Yo lo vi):* Violence and horror defines this picture of people fleeing the attack of French soldiers. What Goya sees and criticises here are the village authorities, sumptuously dressed and obese, but the first to run away, leaving the rest of the population to their fate.

The etching caption *"I saw it"* encapsulates a principle Goya applied throughout his life when the memories of his childhood and youth in Fuendetodos and Zaragoza came flooding back. A person's life and work draw on their roots, which are instrumental in telling the story of their self-development and determining the direction their lives take. There was perhaps a point when Goya believed he had stepped away from his past and reached his future. But no sooner was he there than he redirected his endeavours, setting himself new goals, allowing his work to move on once more, acquiring a new dimension.

In 1810, at the contests which marked the end of the academic year at the Piarists' schools, Manuel Menéndez, a primary school teacher in neighbouring Belchite argued that education should begin "when children have barely started to develop the use of reason," and had this to say about the essay-writing competition:

> This is a most powerful reason to establish wise but cautious competition between essays, however childish. However, it also has other known benefits, for an innate love of celebrity inspires [in children] imperceptible feelings of honour and application to Study, and a desire to win applause by taking this path.

Self-fulfilment could be attained by developing the use of reason, but also in striving for celebrity, which can bestow a sense of wellbeing that goes beyond private pleasures. Such an integral and extensive delight has no comparison and is, according to Ortega y Gasset (1962) what we call happiness. It is perhaps that moment of fame and happiness which Goya later experienced and describes in a letter to Zapater:

> If I had more time, I would tell you about the honour I was given by the king, the prince and the princess, and which I received, by the grace of God, when I showed them four paintings, and kissed their hands; and I had never felt so much joy, and I tell you that I could wish for nothing more than that they liked my works, than the pleasure they obtained from seeing them, and than the satisfaction attained with the king and even more so with their highnesses. And then afterwards, all

that grandeur, thanks be to God, which neither myself nor my works deserve.

We shall go on to consider those achievements in later chapters.

Chapter 2

Fuendetodos

The first settlers in the Fuendetodos area were Celtiberians, who lived in the city of Contrabia Basilisca, now Botorrita, beside the Huerva River, between the 4th and 1st centuries BC. Excavations have yielded four bronze plates with texts on local legal matters and disputes between neighbours regarding irrigation channels. Bronze No. IV, which was found on the path between Botorrita and Fuendetodos, contains the Iberian alphabet with text in the Celtiberian language.

The Roman villa of La Malena in Azuara, near Fuendetodos, dates from a period of expansion of the Roman Empire which reached its greatest splendour in the late 4th century AD. The Romans extracted fossil stone from quarries in Fuendetodos, and the wheel tracks of the transport carts used to build the Aguas Vivas River dam in Almonacid de la Cuba are still visible. The source is in the Cucalón mountains in Teruel and Aguas Vivas flows into the Ebro River in the hamlet of La Zaida. The dam, which made it possible to control river flooding and has a crest of 34 metres, is the highest that was built in the Roman Empire.

In the 5th century, the Visigoths reached military agreements with the Hispano-Romans to defend them against the Franks and barbarian tribes. With the decline of the Roman Empire, Visigoth power strengthened and in 472 AD, Eurico conquered the city of Cesaraugusta, present-day Zaragoza, which then became part of the Visigoth Kingdom of Toulouse, embarking on a period of cultural and religious splendour comparable to Seville and Toledo. One relic from the Visigoth settlement is the 6th-century acropolis discovered in Varella de Castelar in the hamlet of Codo, twenty-eight kilometres from Fuendetodos.

After the Arab invasion of 711, the settlement of Belsid, now Belchite, grew under the auspices of the Taifa of Zaragoza, with settlements of Berber origin related to the Umayyad dynasty, leading to a dramatic improvement in the network of irrigation channels using water from the Almonacid dam. Arab domination lasted until 1118, when the city of Belchite was conquered by Alfonso I the Battler. A medieval castle, known today as Castle of the Moors, was built in Fuendetodos, and is a Spanish cultural heritage site. The ruins of its masonry walls and four towers with arrow slits remain.

The Crown of Aragón — Corona d'Aragón as it is known in Aragonese — dates to 1035, when Ramiro I proclaimed the Kingdom of Aragón in the area around the river Aragón, whose waters flow from the Astún cirque, in the heart of the Pyrenees, near the town of Jaca. During the *Reconquista*, Gastón IV, French Viscount of Bearne, played an important role and was appointed Lord of Zaragoza, Lord Lieutenant of Barbastro and Uncastillo by Alfonso I who also awarded him the major noble title *ricohombre* of Aragón. In 1095, he took part in the First Crusade, earning the epithet "The Crusader" for his victories in Jerusalem leading French and Aragonese troops. As a tribute, the text of the Lord's Prayer is still displayed in Aragonese in the Pater Noster Church of the Carmelite monastery in Jerusalem, erected on the ruins of the church built by the crusaders to protect the cave visited by Jesus of Nazareth. Gastón IV founded the Kingdom of Jerusalem and, after the city was destroyed by the Mamluks in 1291, the title of king was passed down to different monarchs and is today one of the titles still held by the Spanish monarchy.

When Christian troops reconquered the territory of Fuendetodos, in a bid to attract settlers to the area, King Alfonso I the Battler granted Belchite a municipal charter in 1119, awarding *fueros* — separate codes of laws with special rights and concessions — to those who settled in the vicinity. These included certain prerogatives and privileges for Christian vassals, such as permission to plough uncultivated land to plant crops.

Thus, it was that Fuendetodos was repopulated in the late thirteenth century, as an ecclesiastical fief governed by the Bishop of Zaragoza. In the fourteenth century, it became the temporal fief of the Lords of Fuentes, a title held by the Fernández de Heredia family. In 1224, James I the Conqueror donated the neighbouring town of Codoto to the Cistercian monks of the Monastery of Rueda, near Sástago.

Juan Fernández de Heredia was made Count of Fuentes in 1508, presiding over an area that included the villages of Fuentes de Ebro, Mediana, Fuendetodos, Jaulín, María de Huerva and the Barony of Castelflorit. One of the most powerful figures in Europe and a Grand Master of the Order of Jerusalem, his influence extended to Avignon in France, Rhodes in Greece and to Malta. Goya was acquainted — and had dealings with — the sixteenth Count of Fuentes Atanasio Pignatelli of Aragón and Moncayo, a man of the Enlightenment and encyclopaedist, who died in Bordeaux in 1776. The parish priest of San Gil de Zaragoza described him as an "incorrigible sinner and impious Voltairist."

The name Fuendetodos stands for "everybody's source." According to legend, a feudal lord who owned the local land appropriated the water from an old source for his own exclusive use. He was faced with violent opposition from the local inhabitants who managed to secure the water so it could continue to be used by everybody, without restriction or impediment.

In 1137, the County of Barcelona was incorporated into the Crown of Aragón on the marriage, in Barbastro Cathedral, of Petronila, heir to the throne, with Count Ramón Berenguer IV. After new territories had been conquered and treaties and marriage ties secured, the Kingdoms of Mallorca, Valencia, Sicily, Corsica, Sardinia, and Naples were all brought under the Crown of Aragon, as were the Duchies of Athens and

Neopatras. For almost a century, the royal ensign of the Crown of Aragón — with its four pale gules on a gold background — flew above the Acropolis in Athens. Other Crown territories included Roussillon, Urgel, and Tarbes. Roussillon became part of Aragón in 1172 when it was given to King Alfonso II and recovered by France in 1659 under the Treaty of the Pyrenees. In 1793, Goya painted two portraits of General Antonio Ricardos, born in Barbastro, who in the same year, following Louis XVI's death at the guillotine, entered France with a Hispano-Portuguese army, supported by the English Armada, and occupied Roussillon. Godoy subsequently signed the Peace of Basel in 1795, and Roussillon was returned to France.

During its age of splendour, the seat of the Crown of Aragón was Zaragoza, and Aragonese monarchs were crowned in the Cathedral of San Salvador, known as the Seo. From the thirteenth to sixteenth centuries, the General Court of Aragón met in Monzón Castle. Sigena Monastery and the Royal Pantheon were the custodians of the Crown's archives. In the late sixteenth century, once feudal repopulation was achieved and consolidated, any new ploughing of the land was forbidden, exacerbating the tension between the crop farmers who wished to continue with the practice and the livestock farmers who sought to put a stop to it to preserve their grazing pastures.

At the end of the War of Spanish Succession between Habsburg and Bourbon supporters, Philip V became the first Bourbon king of Spain. Royal authority was strengthened by the *Nueva Planta* Decrees which eliminated the rights and *fueros* of the territories of the Crown of Aragón, with the exception of those of the Arán Valley which had supported him. These decrees, passed between 1707 and 1716, abolished the laws and institutions of the Kingdoms of Aragón, Catalonia, and Valencia. Aragón's *fueros* were repealed and although some Aragonese politicians were able to take up positions in Castile, all of Aragón's representational offices were appointed by the King.

The regional institutions — including the legislative *Cortes*, chartered government, *Justicia Mayor* and Supreme Council of Aragón — were all eliminated and replaced by others subordinate to the Captain General of Aragón and President of the court of law which controlled Aragonese tax collection. Some Aragonese nobility opposed the new situation and, together with the Count of Aranda and José Nicolás de Azara, created the Regionalist Party of Aragón using their leverage in a political "exchange" which enabled them to occupy prominent national positions. The Count of Aranda, for instance, was appointed to lead the Council of Castile by Charles III, and then Dean of the Council of State by Charles IV. The Count's daughter married José María Pignatelli, the eldest son of the Count of Fuentes and Lord of Fuendetodos.

The new policy — structured around the aristocracy, the bourgeoisie, and the clergy — sought to modernize Spanish society, developing industry and culture. Enlightened figures propelled the country down the road towards modernity before they were interrupted by the war against Napoleon. The textiles industry was updated and farming prospered. The growing of vines and olives expanded. Uncultivated land only used for pasture was ploughed up. Hydraulic policy led to the intensification of irrigation. In Aragón, the Tauste Canal and Argüis Dam were completed, and in 1768, Zaragozan captain Juan Moreno Monroy presented Charles III with the Yesa and Bardenas Canal project, the germ of the idea behind the current Yesa Dam which regulates the river Aragón and provides irrigation for both Aragón and Navarra.

In Goya's day, the journey between Fuendetodos and Zaragoza had to be made on a dirt track which went as far as Jaulín, and from there to Botorrita. Here travellers could take a road to Valencia, which was more consolidated and better maintained, running parallel to the Huerva River, and entering Zaragoza in its Torrero district. Transport was by coach, and it would have taken seven hours to cover the seven leagues of a journey often fraught with dangers like the highwaymen Goya painted in his ***Stagecoach Hijacking*** *(Asalto a la diligencia)*.

The Count of Aranda's census of the population of Spain in 1768-1769 puts the total number of "souls" at 9,307,804. In the Spanish territories that had belonged to the Crown of Aragón, it is recorded as 2,276,603, almost a quarter of the total. This also explains the importance of the political representatives of the former Crown territories, their governors, and the people of Aragón at national level. In the Count of Floridablanca's census of 1787, "Fuendetodos" appears as a place with an "Ordinary Mayor of Secular Estate," in other words a mayor appointed directly by the local lord. The population totalled 406, of which 223 were men and 183 women. Madoz's dictionary of 1847 describes the village as:

> Located in hilly territory to the right of River Huerva, beaten by the wind, particularly from the North. Its climate is cold and healthy in winter; the most common diseases are pleurisy and rheumatic pain. It has about 180 houses, including the council and the jail, a Moorish castle, somewhat in ruins, and a boys' school with 60 pupils, with a provision of 21,000 *reales* and a girls' school with 24 pupils in attendance and a provision of 800 *reales*.

Today, Fuendetodos and another fourteen municipalities, make up the region known as Campo de Belchite, a province of Zaragoza in the Autonomous Community (region) of Aragón.

It can be reached from Botorrita — which has an important Iberian archeological site — by skirting the river Huerva, a tributary of the Ebro, or from the pottery town of Muel, crossing the wine-making region of Cariñena or the lands of Belchite, which are rich in bird life and olive oil. Situated in north-west Spain, to the south of the province of Zaragoza, in the extensive Huerva valley, forty-four kilometres from the regional capital, Fuendetodos now has 180 registered citizens — considerably fewer than the 406 in Goya's day.

The gentle slopes of Fuendetodos stretch from the dryland extremes of the central Ebro valley to the semi-arid foothills of the Iberian Mountain System. Annual rainfall is 420 millimetres, allowing for moderately good cereal yields every year, with 2,200 kg/ha for barley. Farm crops also include wheat and rye. On some plots, cereal crops are rotated with grain legumes like chickpeas, beans and lentils or fodder. The wheat grown is organic, with more tolerable gluten levels and a higher protein ratio than in other areas, and a very pleasant taste.

Fuendetodos' pine forests create vast green swathes across the slopes and peaks, in dense or more open formations. Residents use these for firewood on a controlled basis. The village has an altitude of 750 metres, and the highest local peak rises to 875 metres in the Sierra de los Entredichos, which covers an area of 6,200 hectares. Crops and land use are as follows: 2,778 hectares are labour-intensive, 1,782 ha. scrubland, 1,255 ha. Aleppo pine, 285 ha. mixed scrubland and Aleppo pine and 57 ha. vineyards, while the remainder is unproductive. The pines grow on limestone terrain, gypsiferous loams and gypsum, on steep slopes and shallow soils. The diverse flora and fauna of great ecological value have led to the Fuendetodos area becoming part of the European Union's Red Natura 2000. The average annual temperature is about fifteen degrees centigrade with variations in summer and winter. The soil and climate have allowed vineyards and olive groves to be grown in Fuendetodos on smaller, family plots, in contrast to the monocultures found in the nearby wine-producing area of Cariñena, just twenty-five kilometres away, or Belchite, at a distance of some nineteen kilometres, which is given over to the production of olive oil.

Traditionally, sheep and goats were farmed for meat and dairy production, and in Goya's day, livestock was a major source of income for farmers, but this activity is absent today. Hunting continues for partridge, quail, rabbit, and hare, as well as pigeon and turtledove in pine and scrubland, with big game like wild boar, roe deer and ibex in the ravines. These rich hunting grounds were the origin of Goya's passion for a pursuit to which he dedicated many works, like the magnificent **Quail Hunting** (a preparatory drawing for *Hunting Party*), **or Hunter with Dog Carrying a Rabbit** (*Cazador con su perro, que trae un conejo*), set on a hill that could easily be in Fuendetodos.

The snow that falls in winter can remain for several days on the north-facing lands sheltered by the foothills of the Iberian Mountain belt and was another important source of revenue in Fuendetodos. It inspired Goya's tapestry cartoon **The Snowstorm or Winter** (*El invierno o La Nevada*), which depicts a slaughtered pig being transported to the house for the gastronomic ritual known as the "*matanza*" where the fresh meat and charcuterie are seasoned.

This cartoon recalls a cold, snowy day set in the stark landscape of Fuendetodos and features the figures of three people carrying a slaughtered pig that will serve as food reserves for the year ahead. One of these figures was later to become the central motif in the print **Witches' Flight** (*Vuelo de brujas*), where the sad and silent thoughts of the figures take the form of a group of witches in dunces caps dancing in a ring with naked torsos, in this case with no sign of the cold.

This snow was collected and transported to ice pits or ice houses, constructions of Asian and African origin, brought to Spain by Arab and Jewish peoples who perfected the art during the sixteenth to nineteenth centuries. Shaped like cylindrical wells, they were about five metres wide and six meters deep, covered by a cone-shaped dome and corbel vault with a single opening. The building material used was fossil stone, abundant in Fuendetodos, and the base of the pit was prepared with a wooden lattice structure to allow water to drip through when the ice thawed. Once placed in the pit, the layers of snow — sometimes forty centimetres thick — were pressed and separated with straw to transform them into blocks of ice. The ice was used for the cold storage of medicines and perishable foodstuffs.

In Spain, the cost of ice was set by the two major production centres: Granada in Andalusia and Fuendetodos in Aragón, and a rudimentary inter-professional ice collaboration was created. A set price per-hectare was paid to owners of the land where the snow was deposited, including the cost of transporting it to the ice pits, in keeping with specific standards of quality and cleanliness. The cost of the ice was established in relation to storage time, the cost of paying off the building of the ice structure, the daily wages for stacking the snow in layers protected by straw until it changed into ice, the wages paid for its removal and nocturnal transportation in carts to Zaragoza. A verbal deal was struck with the buyers, setting a price for ice supplies all year round.

There were twenty-one ice pits in Fuendetodos, and Goya's grandfather owned one of them, the Culroya. His main customers were the monks of the Charterhouse of Aula Dei, near Zaragoza. It was in this charterhouse, between 1772 and 1774, where the Prior Fray Félix Salcedo hired Goya to paint the church walls, at the age of 28, with monumental frescoes on the Life of the Virgin.

The Culroya ice pit has since been restored and can be visited. It is effectively a museum to the system used before present-day refrigerators were invented to preserve food and other items. There is a spiral staircase leading down to the bottom of the pit. La Roza and El Calvario ice pits still preserve part of their initial structure. One of the smaller pits, in the Tío Faustino limestone quarry, was still used for ice in the nineteen fifties and also to obtain chalk throughout the twentieth century.

Today, another icehouse is being restored as a Wind Museum. Fuendetodos has recently become involved in the promotion of renewable energies and a number of wind farms have been set up, with the turbines positioned to minimize their environmental impact.

There are also quarries in the vicinity of Fuendetodos which contain fossil stone formed millions of years ago in the Middle Miocene when the sea covered the area and in which the fossilized remains of small shells can still be found. The tracks of the Roman carts which transported the limestone to build Zaragoza's city walls are visible in the quarry near Fuente Vieja.

Fossil stone was and is used to build housing façades and hydraulic structures, like the Stone Bridge over the River Ebro in Zaragoza and the dam in the neighbouring village of Almonacid de la Sierra. It was also used in large-scale buildings like the Pilar and Seo Cathedrals in Zaragoza in the seventeenth and eighteenth centuries.

Flint quarries have emerged amidst the white limestone, which are also from the Miocene. Flint was used to build the Camino Viejo — or Old Road — to circumnavigate the abrupt slopes of the earlier paths where the gradient is steep, and which were difficult to negotiate by horse-drawn cart.

Fuendetodos farmers also earned income from the forested areas of pine, savin and kermes oak, which were used for resin, timber and firewood, and the production of charcoal. There was also small-scale limestone and gypsum production and a weaver on the outskirts of town, on the road to Villanueva de Huerva. In Goya's day, the town council was responsible for forestry exploitation, and in 1761, leased woodland for sixty-year terms, taking charge of care and maintenance.

The doctor visited Belchite once a week, except in an emergency when he had to be sent for. Minor ailments were treated with home remedies like milk with honey taken from hives located in meadows of rosemary or sage, or bran poultices. Any broken bones would be temporarily fixed by a village healer until the doctor arrived. The post was delivered twice a week.

Tithes were collected by the Lord of Fuendetodos,[3] the sixteenth Count of Fuentes who, from 1745 and during Goya's time, was Juan Joaquín Atanasio Pignatelli de Aragón y Moncayo, brother of Ramón. A cathedral canon and important politician in Zaragoza, Ramón was also the promoter of Aragon's Imperial Canal, and founder of the *Real Sociedad Económica de Amigos del País*, a society that was part of the movement to stimulate economic and intellectual development. Another of the count's brothers was José, a Jesuit who forced to leave Spain for Rome, where he died in 1881 and was buried in the Church of the Gesù alongside the Jesuit Fathers. He was canonized in 1954 by Pope Pius XII.

The "sunken church" of Our Lady of Villares, the original medieval parish church until 1728 which then became the Chapel of Our Lord of the Burial, has been in ruins since the nineteenth century. Recent excavations in May 2019 revealed the

---

[3]   A tax of 10% of income paid to the feudal lord.

font where Goya's mother, Gracia Lucientes, was christened and it is possible that members of her family were buried here.

The Church of Our Lady of the Assumption, in the highest part of town, overlooking the village, was built in the seventeenth century, originally in the Baroque style. Later in 1728, it became the Neoclassical parish church. As we have seen, it was here on the doors of the reliquary that Goya painted one of his first works. The church was later destroyed in the Spanish Civil War and rebuilt in Neo-Mudéjar style in 1960. Inside is the font where Goya was baptized, made from marbled granite and with a base of black stone from nearby Calatorao, and restored to its original Baroque style.

First fruits[4] were secularized and began to be collected and managed by the Council of Fuendetodos, which also took care of the running and maintenance of the church. Goya's father was responsible for the gilding of its main altarpiece. At that time, Goya's future father-in-law Miguel Lucientes, was mayor and head of the Council. On a pastoral visit in 1746, the Archbishop of Zaragoza, Añoa y Basto, praised the gilding for its beauty and splendid execution.

In the province of Zaragoza in the mid-nineteenth century, all the local schools were primarily devoted to the education of boys. Girls' schools barely made up twenty-three per cent of the total and there was, of course, no such thing as mixed schools. But the mere fact that in Fuendetodos, there were two — one for boys and one for girls — is indicative of the educational level in the province as a whole and was due in part to the availability of enough resources to maintain both. Apart from the Council, funding also came from parents, common farmland revenue and a payment made by the Lord of Fuendetodos.

---

[4]   First fruits were the part of the harvest offered to the church in recognition of God's generosity.

The comparatively small number of girls attending school can partly be attributed to the lack of importance which society and rural families attached to their daughters' studies. Insufficient funding for the creation and maintenance of school buildings and teachers' salaries was another reason, hence the need for a parental contribution. Council funding was greater for boys' schools and families therefore had to pay a good deal more to make up the shortfall for their daughters. As a result, many only sent their sons. On top of that, girls had to work more in the home, taking on domestic chores and looking after their siblings so their mothers could work in the fields. Boys missed school more occasionally, when there was extra work on the farm, such as during the cereal harvest season.

Boys learned to read and write, grammar, arithmetic, and spelling, whereas girls were taught different subjects. The regulation established by Charles III in 1783 laid down the basis for the teaching of manual skills "starting with the easiest such as girdles, knitting, crochet, sampling, hemming and sewing, followed by a more refined kind of sewing, embroidery and lace-making." Emilia Pardo Bazán wrote that, in the eighteenth century, it was considered dangerous to teach girls the alphabet because, "if they knew how to read, it would have been easy for them to maintain correspondence with their beaux."

Goya's first contact with painting and drawing was at school in Fuendetodos. His picture *La letra con sangre entra* was painted around 1780 and depicts a schoolroom where the teacher is punishing a pupil. It is sometimes translated *"With pain comes gain"* but might perhaps more accurately be translated as *"Spare the rod and spoil the child!"*

Some aspects of the education Goya would have received can be inferred from the poster shown below for a competition organized in Belchite in 1801, which would have involved the Piarist Schools. It lists the subjects the pupils had to enter:

Competition organized in Belchite in 1801 with English translation

PUBLICOS EXERCICIOS

DE RELIGION CHRISTIANA,

BUENA CRIANZA

LEER; ESCRIBIR; ORTOGRAFÍA, I AGRICULTURA,

CONQUE SE ALIENTAN

A MAIORES EMPEÑOS, LOS NIÑOS DE LA

ESCUELA REAL

DE LA M.N., I M.L. VILLA DE BELCHITE,

DIRIGIDOS

POR SU MAESTRO D. MANUEL MENENDEZ,

EXAMINADO

POR EL REAL COLEGIO ACADÉMICO MATRITENSE,

APROVADO

POR EL REAL I SUPREMO CONSEJO DE CASTILLA,

I SE CONSAGRAN

AL M.I. AYUNTAMIENTO DE LA MISMA,

LOS QUE SE CELEBRARÁN

En la Iglesia Parroquial de ella, en

el día 17 de noviembre de 1.801

CON LICENCIA

PUBLIC EXERCISES

OF CHRISTIAN RELIGION,

GOOD BREEDING

READING; WRITING; SPELLING & FARMING,

TO ENCOURAGE

GREATER EFFORT AMONG THE CHILDREN OF THE

ROYAL SCHOOL

OF THE MOST NOBLE & LOYAL TOWN OF BELCHITE, DIRECTED

BY THEIR TEACHER D. MANUEL MENENDEZ,

EXAMINED

BY THE ROYAL ACADEMIC COLLEGE OF MADID

APPROVED

BY THE ROYAL COUNCIL OF CASTILE,

BEING ASSIGNED

TO THE MOST ILLUSTRIOUS COUNCIL OF THAT TOWN,

AND TAKING PLACE

In its Parish Church, on the 17th day of November 1801

UNDER LICENCE

The following is a quotation taken from the competition exercises:

- Definition of the four parts of the world
- Colloquium in verse on the instruction every child should receive, and the meaning of holy mass
- Samaniego's fables
- A question on music
- Reading in Latin of the lessons indicated
- Reading in Castilian
- Definitions and rules on the art of writing
- Notices that have been designed in school for this purpose
- Castilian spelling and punctuation
- Summaries of Pinton's historical catechism
- Farming dialogue
- All the centuries contained in Father De Isla's History of Spain in verse
- Battle of two hundred questions from the "Compendium of Christian Doctrine" taught in Piarist Schools
- Dialogue on politics and good breeding

Finally, it indicates that "victory" for the winner will be followed by a coronation and the awarding of a silver medal.

Two aspects of this interesting list — identical in all the schools in the area, including Fuendetodos — are worth mentioning. The first was that children's education was geared to the development of the 'self' as an individual, as described at the beginning of this book, and that this was connected to the notion of attaining self-fulfilment and happiness through achievement on the terms quoted in his letter to Zapater on his first audience with the king and royal family. The second is the reference to the notices the children had to design at school "for this purpose", suggesting that they were also taught the art of drawing, at least while the competition was underway.

Later, in the Constitution of 1812 passed by the Cortes of Cádiz, primary education became more standardized, and an order was issued to establish schools all over Spain which would teach reading, writing and arithmetic, the Catholic catechism, and a brief exposition of civil obligations. The *Gaceta de Madrid* — the Official Gazette — of 9 August 1821 describes the subjects to be taught in the new school in Plaza Antón Martín which essentially coincides with those listed for Belchite at the time.

The physiocratic theory of the day advocated that a country's wealth be based on agriculture and natural resources. Population growth required the production of more food. Consequently, the ploughing of more communal or uncultivated land and of the property of great lords began to be permitted, as was the chopping down of forests. New farming techniques were introduced, with oxen replaced by faster working mules and the use of organic fertilizer from livestock. This was a foretaste of the subsequent mechanization that would accelerate at the turn of the century, enabling the larger-scale tilling of the land and creating large agricultural estates with substantial capital input, replacing human and animal labour, and forcing many farmhands to migrate to the city.

The ploughing of communal land created conflict between farmers, municipalities, and the aristocratic landowners, as the space owned by farmers increased. Setting boundaries was always complicated and the ploughmen were often influenced by those who stood to profit from the ploughing, particularly people in positions of authority who wished to extend their farmlands. The situation also benefitted farmers in Fuendetodos, including the Lucientes family, providing them with a substantial annual income.

In Aragón, the word *roturados* is still used to refer to previously uncultivated fields owned by large landowners, usually the local council, which farmers have put into production. The concept dates to the Visigoth era when what was known as the "right to *escalio*" allowed local residents to break up untilled land. This right was included in the *fueros* of the Kingdom of Aragón of 1247 without any restriction except the obligation to continue to cultivate the land ploughed. This right was diluted by subsequent regulations which required a council permit to plough land and the payment of an annual levy. In the eighteenth century, around the time when Goya was born, several attempts were made to ascertain the exact status of ploughed land in Spain and to regulate its use with laws like the decrees of 1737 and 1748.The second of these decrees banned ploughing and required meadows cultivated between 1728 and 1748 be restored to pastureland. It was no easy matter to determine how each plot of land should be categorized, as many farmers alleged they had been ploughing the land since before 1728. Moreover, surveyors were often in cahoots with the ploughmen, especially when these were local authorities like the mayor and town councillors.

It became virtually impossible for people to distinguish the boundaries of ploughed fields from their own land, owing to the vehement opposition of farmworkers and their failure to cooperate. Moreover, the livestock farmers formed a powerful association called the Mesta which did not accept property deeds because they were of the view that farmers had already included grazing land on their own properties, which often led to further conflict. This was undoubtedly one of the reasons why Goya's parents and grandparents remained in the village: it meant they were on site to defend the land they had tilled and preserve it as part of their estate.

In Albarracín, a village near Fuendetodos, the Mesta authority in charge of ensuring the laws were observed, referred to the "great distaste" towards reception of and compliance with the Royal Orders on the treatment of ploughed land, claiming these were contrary to Aragón's special *fuero* laws. But the policy, which had been designed to benefit livestock farmers, proved to be of no avail, and land continued to be cultivated to grow more cereal. Under Charles III, agricultural policy continued to favour the spread of crops and the ploughing of the land to cater for a growing population. Ploughing was legalized again, and a blind eye was turned to illegal ploughing. Ownership could be asserted for life if the land was tilled. Permits expired if no crops were grown for six years; the land had to be farmed directly rather than by leasing out the land, and neither transfer nor sale to outsiders was allowed. In short, the expanse of ploughed land grew dramatically in the eighteenth century.

Goya did not engage with the subject of ploughed land that was so important to his family's economic situation or take sides in the conflict over its use. For one thing, he only lived in Fuendetodos for a few years. His own professional activities enabled him to earn a living without the need to resort to farm revenue, and later in Madrid, he would live among some of the biggest owners of Spanish farmland, like the Pignatellis, the Albas and the Osunas, who also became his patrons. The world of farming was chiefly of interest to him to the extent that it represented contact with nature, and in the richness and diversity of its rural traditions.

Even today there are municipalities in Aragón where the ploughed land is not owned by those who farm it. In the late twentieth century, this situation was settled in the landmark case of Sástago,[5] a village with 25,000 hectares on the banks of the river Ebro, not far from Fuendetodos, which was awarded its Village Charter in 1614 by the Count of Sástago, whose family had received the dominion in 1223 from James I the Conqueror.

After the arduous task of marking the boundaries, ploughed, and cultivated rural land in the village was classified as the property of the Count, the Council, or the farmers. Once demarcated, a land bank was formed from the ploughed earth and new partitioning was undertaken, establishing a maximum of 120 hectares for the large landowners, and joining plots of up to 120 hectares — the area considered economically viable for a farm estate — for small landholders, either individually or collectively. This redistribution was accompanied by soft loans to facilitate access to the ownership of ploughed land, and by a land consolidation process to allow for farms of adequate size and more efficient design that could subsequently be transformed into irrigated land. The late nineteenth century brought water from the Upper Aragón irrigation system, under the auspices of Joaquín Costa, and this was consolidated by law in 1911.

But let us return to Francisco de Goya. Born at number 15, Calle de la Alhóndiga in Fuendetodos on 30 March 1746, he was baptized the following day in the parish church of La Ascensión, the son of Braulio José Goya y Franques and Gracia Lucientes y Salvador. His mother's family came from the same village, where his grandparents lived comfortably from their farmland. His baptism certificate in Fuendetodos church reads as follows:

> On the thirty-first of March, seventeen hundred and for-
> ty-six, I the undersigned vicar, baptised this child born on the

---

5   Carlos Arroyos J. Ordenación de explotaciones en la Comarca de Sástago. Instituto Nacional de Reforma y Desarrollo Agrario (IRYDA). Report no.25. 1978

day immediately before this one, as the legitimate son of José Goya and Gracia Lucientes, legitimately married inhabitants of this parish and resident in Zaragoza; he has been named Francisco Joseph Goya; his godmother was Francisca de Grasa, of this Parish, maiden daughter of Miguel Lucientes and Gracia María Salvador, whom I notified of the spiritual kinship into which she has entered with the baptized child and the obligation to teach him the Christian Doctrine in the absence of his parents; and for the sake of Truth, I hereby conduct and sign this Present Document in FuendeTodos, on the aforesaid date, month and year. Reverend José Ximeno, Vicar.

Goya was named José after his father and Francisco as a tribute to his godmother, Francisca. He was born in the year of the death of Spain's first Bourbon king, Philip V, when his second son, Ferdinand VI came to the throne, although these events would have been remote for Goya's family in Fuendetodos and may possibly even have gone unnoticed.

As we shall see in greater detail, Goya's mother had a house in Fuendetodos, and his grandparents had quite considerable farm property, so they could live untouched by the serious food shortages experienced in Zaragoza and by the popular uprisings demanding flour and improved living conditions in the city. In addition, their children could be educated for free in the excellent schools in Fuendetodos, at least until the end of primary, whereas private schooling in Zaragoza would have been beyond their reach.

Goya later moved to Zaragoza, where he was living in 1808 when the French were expelled in the first siege of the city. During the second siege at the end of that year, however, he feared French reactions to his sketches for "The Disasters of War", and returned to seek refuge in Fuendetodos, where he would have relived his early childhood memories.

According to Zapater's biography (1868), the residents of Fuendetodos who were Goya's contemporaries recalled that last visit to Fuendetodos in 1808. He was already deaf by that time and used signing with an alphabet he had invented to communicate with a servant he had brought with him. The biography also refers to his having moved away from Fuendetodos where "there was nothing left [...] he could learn as a painter." Goya would have felt safer and more protected in his home village, where he was welcomed, even though it meant putting aside the comforts and social life of the city. But his artistic vocation, which required an ongoing learning process, led to his definitive departure.

Over the years, Goya and his childhood in Fuendetodos have been commemorated in many different ways. The village, as we have seen, had a defining impact on the artist's sense of self and his artistic formation. In 1913, the Basque painter Ignacio Zuloaga and a group of friends set up a commemorative plaque in Fuendetodos sculpted by Dionisio Lasuén. Goya's house and museum at 15, Calle de la Alhóndiga opened to the public in 1917, having been purchased by Zuloaga a year earlier. The marble plaque on the façade contains the following text:

English translation of the marble plaque
on Goya House and Museum

THIS HUMBLE ABODE,
WAS THE BIRTHPLACE OF THE
DISTINGUISHED PAINTER
FRANCISCO DE GOYA Y LUCIENTES,
BRINGING HONOUR TO HIS
HOMELAND AND AWE TO ART

30 March 1746 to 16 April 1828

WITH THE ADMIRATION OF ALL OF US
TRIBUTE IS PAID TO HIS MEMORY

In October 1920, a bronze bust sculpted free of charge by Julio Antonio and his pupil Salazar was unveiled on a monolith in the church square. The monolith — paid for by public subscription — comprises a three-metre-high rectangular column of unpolished green jasper quarried in the nearby village of Codos, and reads as follows:

English translation of the inscription on the bronze
bust of Goya in the church square of Fuendetodos
SO THAT THE SPIRIT OF THE IMMORTAL
ARTIST, WHOSE GLORY HAS SPREAD
ALL OVER THE WORLD, MAY LIVE ON IN
THE VILLAGE WHERE HE WAS BORN

IGNACIO ZULOAGA & FRIENDS HEREBY
ERECT THIS MONUMENT

19 OCTOBER 1920

In 1978, on the anniversary of the painter's death in Bordeaux, a wrought iron bust of Goya, made by the Aragonese artist from Teruel, José Gonzalvo Vives, was installed in the square in front of Goya's birthplace. In 1982, Goya's birthplace was declared an Artistic and Historical Monument.

Fuendetodos Today

The village's small population of 180 contrasts with a dynamic cultural scene, where tourists, artists and researchers frequent its charming streets and historical buildings. Traditional buildings retain their aesthetic appeal, and there are valuable examples of medieval, Arab, Mudéjar, Renaissance and eighteenth-century architecture which have left their mark on the street layout. The village is still divided into two neighbourhoods, a higher part, known as the *Barrio Alto* and a lower one, the *Barrio Bajo*.

The upper part of the village converges on the Plaza de Aragón. Its elegantly proportioned houses have large balconies and doors with semi-circular arches dating from the seventeenth and eighteenth centuries. Steps lead up to the church and the Plaza de la Constitución, which leads to the ruins of a palace and masonry walls with pointed arches from the transition to Gothic style. There are also a large number of Renaissance buildings with arched galleries.

To the north of the village, in Calle Cortes de Aragón, are the ruins of the Moorish Castle, which provide a vantage point from which to gaze on the panorama Goya himself would have contemplated as a boy and which he remained a lifelong memory for him. The current church, between the two neighbourhoods, replaced the one that was destroyed in the Spanish Civil War between 1936 and 1939. It remains the religious, social, and physical heart of the village and was a constant landmark in Goya's paintings. In ***The Third of May,*** for instance, it stands like a silent, wounded witness to the atrocities taking place. This memory of Goya's has been observed by several authors. Hugh Thomas (1979), for instance, saw the hill to the left behind the main figures as a depiction of the Fuendetodos landscape, and interpreted the church building on the right as a symbol of hope: a permanent and indestructible representation of values.

Fuendetodos holds its local festival on 24 August in honour of its patron Saint Bartholomew, and the council organizes cultural activities every year. Goya's birthday is celebrated from 30 March to mid-April and was of particular significance in 2021 on the 275th anniversary. What is known today as the Old Fountain is the source which is said to have given the village its name. This spring came to light during medieval excavations in the rock and can be accessed by a Gothic gateway that has recently been restored. Fuendetodos is not a wealthy village, firstly because its lands are unirrigated, which reduces yields and also because, until recently, farming was the only economic activity.

However, recent initiatives — listed below — are helping to improve the lives of the local population and to make different aspects of Goya's life and work more widely known.

- Improvement of road links to allow better access to the village and encourage tourism.
- The building of a hotel, a hostel, several cottage rentals, restaurants and the restoration of kiln from Goya's day, providing visitors with accommodation and traditional food.
- A wind farm, with minimal environmental impact, has been installed with total installed power capacity of 130 megawatts. This has significantly contributed to local revenue.
- The establishment of the Fundación Goya in Aragón, a private foundation based on a public initiative by the Aragón regional government, with its head office in Zaragoza. It has a magnificent online catalogue of the painter's work and promotes exhibitions and cultural activities on the subject of Goya.

- The Goya-Fuendetodos Cultural Consortium, under the auspices of the Provincial Council, with its head office in Zaragoza, organises exhibitions on the artist's work and helps run the Print Museum in Fuendetodos, Goya's birthplace and the Zuloaga Temporary Exhibition Centre. Since 1966, the Zuloaga Centre, in the building beside Goya's birthplace, houses temporary graphic art exhibitions, both historical and contemporary. In 2019 it hosted "Architectural Monuments of Spain" in partnership with the San Fernando Royal Academy of Fine Arts, offering chance to see fifty prints from this extraordinary nineteenth-century publishing project. An exhibition featuring forty-seven twenty-first-century Spanish and international artists entitled ***"Los Disparates (Follies) of Fuendetodos 2000-2020"*** was on show here until September 2020. The exhibition brought together all the works — some created in the village itself — based on Goya's ***Follies*** print series, using different graphic techniques.
- The Print Museum, which opened in 1989, houses the series ***Los Caprichos*** and ***The Disasters of War***. Sadly, building work at the new Goya Museum of Contemporary Print in Fuendetodos has been halted due to lack of funding. The aim is for this modular building to become a leading centre for Spanish and international graphic art, with permanent and temporary exhibitions rooms and an etching and engraving research and interpretation centre. Among the activities planned is an international two-month postgraduate course in printmaking for international students taught by prominent teachers, including some who have already given lectures and exhibited work in Fuendetodos, such as the Nobel-Prize-winning author Günter Grass, printmakers Monir, Zachrisson, John Berger, Masao Yamamoto, Spanish

artists José Beulas, Arroyo, Guinovart, José Manuel Broto, Victor Mira and Spanish National Design Award winner Isidro Ferrer to name a few. The new museum will house a library on Goya and a philatelic section for physical and digital viewing of the vast number of stamps that have been dedicated to Goya.

- A commemorative walk or *romería* is organized each year to celebrate the pilgrimage made by Zuloaga and a group of artist and historian friends in 1913 from Apartadero de la Princesa, ten kilometres from the village, which concluded with a gala performance in the Church of Our Lady of the Assumption, with leading figures from the world of opera such as baritone Isaac Galán.

- Fundación Fuendetodos-Goya was created in 2008 to promote building of the new Print Museum and organizes a variety of training, education, and outreach activities each year about Goya's work.

- The Antonio Saura Graphic Arts Studio was created in 1994 to provide graphic art training courses and professional gatherings. The 24th edition in 2020 included a course in electrolytic etching, directed by Silvia Pagliano, aquatinting on copper plate taught by Pascual Adolfo and mokurito lithography, coordinated by Verónica Domingo.

- The Fuendeverde Nature Space is located in a two-storey bioclimatic building owned by the council and has a lecture room on the ground floor for talks and workshops on environmental themes aimed at biologists. On the top floor, a series of panels and dioramas display some of the four hundred species of flora and fauna which inhabit the *foces* or ravines of Fuendetodos.[6]

---

[6] The *foces* are steep ravines where wind and water erosion have carved the limestone in this arid region, leaving damper areas of shade protected

- The Fuendeverde Association's Environmental Education Programme offers activities on the rich biodiversity of the local countryside with well-signposted hiking, biking, and riding trails to follow the paths Goya himself would have trodden.

Cultural and sporting activities related to Goya are also organized all year round:

- A Street Art show where the village is turned into an outdoor art gallery featuring work of different artists on the façades, walls, and doors of buildings. There are plans for an open-air exhibition with sculptures like the wrought-iron creations by local artist Pascual López.
- The Huesca Astronomy Group, in partnership with Fuendetodos council and the Goya Association, organizes stargazing with the telescope installed on what used to be a threshing ground, the *"Era del Catalán"*, offering superb views of the night skies. Photographer M. Membrado took some magnificent pictures from Sierra del Currú of the Neowise comet in July 2020 with its sweeping dust trail in shades of red and blue-glowing ions.

---

from the bitter *cierzo* wind, permitting diverse flora and fauna to flourish. Of the total twenty-three gullies, the biggest — known as *Hoz Mayor* or Great Gorge — covers a distance of about two kilometres and is classified by the European Union as a Site of Ecological Interest. The flora is primarily composed of copses of maple, hackberry, terebinth, snowy Mespilus, fern and rock flora. Wildlife includes the Egyptian vulture — an icon of Fuendetodos — birds of prey such as the griffon vulture, eagle owl and long-eared owl, kites, little owl, kestrel and short-toed eagle, as well as sparrows, swallows, badgers and voles. Game includes wild boar, ibex, fox, red-legged partridge, and rabbit. Goya depicted many of these animals in his paintings and prints, like *The Sleep of Reason Produces Monsters* and *Volaverunt*.

- The Goya rural short film festival and photography rally is held yearly, with prizes for the top three entries in both categories.
- The sports park for adults and children, and a botanical garden close to Balsa del Lugar, which is now a lake with ducks and swans. The recreation area has swimming pools, a five-a-side football field, basketball and paddle tennis court, and a children's playground.
- The Espacio Fuendetodos holds events including the Baluarte Aragonés *jota* dances, publishes the Nueva Alaska magazine, and organizes concerts of popular and traditional songs like those sung and composed by Carmen París.

Currently missing from the programme is a permanent screening of the many films and documentaries dedicated to Goya.

But although much remains to be done, all these events have made Goya's birthplace Fuendetodos a hub for tens of thousands of people interested in finding out more about the life and experiences of the genius from Aragón and discovering his roots and childhood. Fuendetodos also deserves a special place in the Sustainable Development Programmes co-financed by the European Union to improve the quality of life in rural areas, coordinated by the structural and investment funds. The diversification of its economy and particularly, of tourist-related activities would help to shine a light on the universal figure of Francisco de Goya.

Chapter 3

Goya y Lucientes

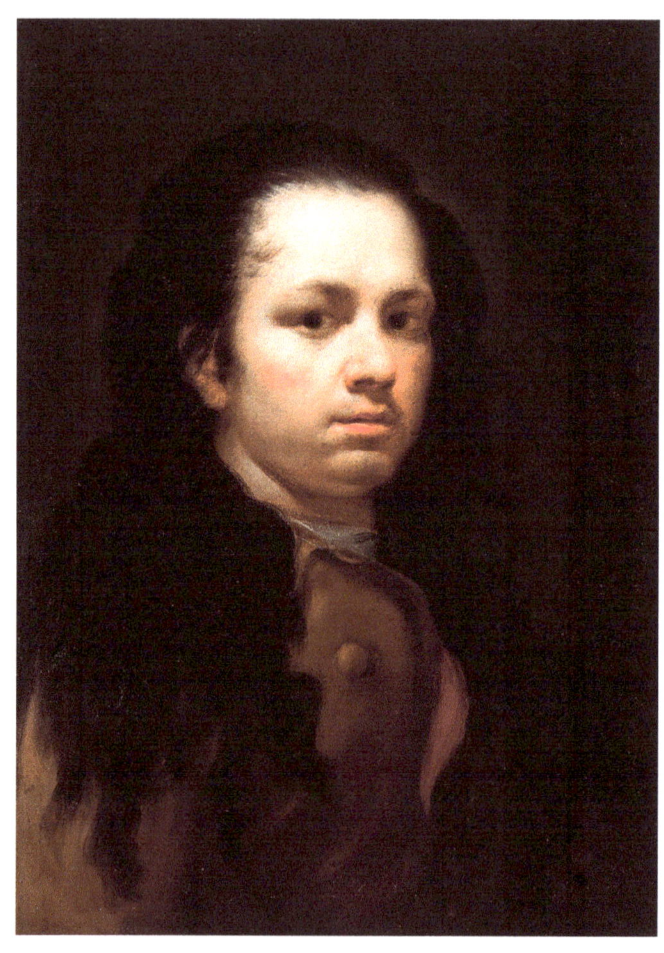

Francisco de Goya y Lucientes. Self-portrait.
© Goya Museum. Fundación Ibercaja

In the year 800, Charlemagne was crowned Holy Roman Emperor by Pope Leo III in Rome. His sarcophagus, in the Palatine Cathedral of Aachen, depicts the legend in which Saint James the Apostle appears to Charlemagne and informs him that he has been chosen to liberate European land from the Muslims, calling on the emperor to visit his tomb in Galicia. Charlemagne then embarked on his journey to the saint's tomb in Santiago de Compostela.

This marked the beginning of the pilgrims' route called the Camino de Santiago or the "Way of Saint James", and more specifically the "French Way", known as the Camino de las Estrellas, the Way of the Stars. From then on, routes developed all over France and other European countries, entering Spain via Roncesvalles from Saint Jean Pied de Port, and across Somport or the Canfranc Pass in Jaca from Oloron. From there, they all followed the path that leads to Santiago de Compostela. From Aachen, this is more than 1,900 kilometres away, with adjoining routes that have been travelled by millions of pilgrims over the centuries. The route is marked by thousands of churches, basilicas, cathedrals, hospitals and monasteries in the towns and villages the Camino crosses.

The eleventh century saw the rebuilding of the Benedictine monastery of Cluny in Burgundy — a German region until 1022 when it became French territory — which was the largest place of worship in Christendom. Its style was Romanesque, reflecting the new revolutionary spirit that prevailed in the West, where there was a desire for renewal. Avoiding earlier opulence, it recalled ancient Roman basilicas, resorting to bare stone, which was perceived as the noblest material to accompany prayer, in a setting where the light was subdued and where silence reigned, as Rodin expressed it (1914).

This regeneration in architectural activity, which led both to new constructions and the renovation of religious and aristocratic buildings, continued with Gothic style between the fourteenth and sixteenth centuries. Unlike today, religious buildings were utterly defined by spirituality, and their architectural elements set the guidelines and served as a model for civil and secular structures. Let us revisit some of the major works from that time.

The first Romanesque church in Spain was the Cathedral of Saint Peter in Jaca. Built in 1077 in the design of a basilica with three naves and apses, it was the episcopal see in what the capital of the Kingdom of Aragon was then. Richly sculpted, its original decoration of Jaca chequer reappears in numerous buildings along the Way of Saint James.

Santiago de Compostela Cathedral, begun in 1078, was and continues to be the ultimate destination for pilgrims throughout Christendom. Characterized by its crossing of three impressive, vaulted naves supported directly on galleries, it can be entered through the beautiful, and recently restored, Portico of Glory, with its dynamic, polychrome figures that contrast with the rigidity of previous styles.

This was followed by San Juan de la Peña, with its beautiful cloister and magnificent capitals carved beneath the rock, and the Benedictine Monastery of Leyre, where the Romanesque church became the mausoleum of the ancient kings of Navarra. The austere Cistercian Abbey of Poblet, which dates from 1153, with its three naves and ambulatories, was consecrated as the royal mausoleum of the Crown of Aragon. The Cathedral of Santo Domingo de la Calzada, built in 1158, contains both the tomb of Saint Dominic of the Causeway, and a small henhouse which was built later in the Gothic style and permanently houses chickens to commemorate the miracle of the rooster and the hen. The current Church of Saint Dominic in Soria, built in

1170, was the site of the wedding between Alfonso VIII and Eleonor of England, who became Queen of Castile. Its façade is undoubtedly the most beautiful and artistic example of Spanish Romanesque, with its four archivolts depicting biblical scenes, dominated by a splendid rosette.

Where civil construction is concerned, the "Queen's Bridge" in Puente de la Reina is particularly outstanding. This is where the two roads entering Spain via the Roncesvalles and Somport passes merge and continue to Santiago de Compostela. This slender Romanesque bridge over the river Aragon, built in the eleventh century, consists of seven arches supported by five pillars.

Gothic style was originally represented in Spain by three spectacular cathedrals which follow the essence and style of the French Gothic found in Paris and Reims, where parts of the walls are replaced by stained glass windows through which the light enters, recalling the radiance of celestial Jerusalem. Abutments and flying buttresses are used to bear the weight. These are the Cathedral of Santa Maria de la Regla in León, on which work began in 1205; the Cathedral of Burgos, dedicated to Saint Mary, of 1221; and the Cathedral of San Salvador in Oviedo, also from the thirteenth century, which was built on the pre-Romanesque structures of the earlier church and within which important relics, including a Holy Shroud, are kept.

Thus, from the eleventh to the late sixteenth century, Europe became an immense workshop for carving stone, where hundreds of families of stonemasons, craftsmen and master builders were involved in the construction of countless churches, monasteries, hospitals and other military and civil works in Romanesque and Gothic style, all along the Camino de Santiago in countries like Belgium, France, Germany, and Portugal, as well as Spain.

I uphold the hypothesis that one of these families, whose surname was Goyet, Goia or Goyaa, and originally came from Flemish Brabant or France, was gradually moving southwards and eventually turned up — with the hispanized name Goya — on the 1578 census in Zerain, a village in Guipuzcoa traversed by the Way of Saint James, with a large quarry for the highly sought-after brownstone used in the construction of churches and noble buildings.

The first reference in Spain to the surname Goya was found in a document in Huesca from the year 1400, which mentions one Juan del Grado y Bona de Goya buying houses for the equivalent of 1100 Jaca sous.[7] However, there is no evidence that this man was either a stone mason or an ancestor of Goya.

The Flemish hypothesis is not easy to confirm without knowing the journey taken by the family of stone masons bearing this surname. It would require the study of the population censuses where Romanesque and Gothic buildings were built in Belgium, France and Spain, or a detailed cryptographic study of the monuments built during this lengthy period, to detect their mason's marks along the route to Zerain in Guipúzcoa. Other surnames originating from the Flemish Brabant certainly exist in Spain: Charlez in Aragon, and Becker — hispanized to 'Bécquer' by the Andalusian poet Gustavo Adolfo — are cases in point. The lack of historical data about the family before the record in Zerain also prevented Goya from proving his noble background, a requirement to become a court painter. It was therefore to the recognized nobility of his maternal family tree that he resorted to obtain the necessary credentials.

---

[7] Information obtained from the Archivo Histórico Nacional. A *sueldo jaqués* or 'Jaca sou' is a currency unit that was used in Aragón at that time

In 1567, Francisco's ancestor Pedro de Goya appeared on the census in Zerain when he married Mariana Echeandía and went to reside in the small village of Mantxolatxiki. The Goya family of stone masons carved the coveted brownstone from Mount Arripillata and were also instructors at a stone carving workshop for young apprentices. The continuation of this family — Goya's ancestors — is well documented right up to his arrival in Fuendetodos, as we shall see.

From Zerain, the Goya family went to live in Fuentes de Jiloca in 1625, where Domingo Goya, a master builder by profession, built the church tower. In 1632, Domingo's son Pedro was born in Zaragoza, and later became the father of Pedro Felipe, who was baptized in the Zaragoza's Church of Saint Philip. He served as a royal notary, was made *hidalgo* by Royal Provision, and belonged to the noble militia known as the *Real Maestranza de Caballería*. The substantial earnings from his trade enabled him to buy three adjacent houses on the street called Morería Cerrada.

Pedro Felipe's son Jose Goya was baptized in the Parish Church of San Gil in Zaragoza. He worked as a gilder and in 1736 married Gracia Lucientes from Fuendetodos where, on 30 March 1746, their famous Aragonese son, Francisco José de Goya y Lucientes was born.

The Lucientes family came from the eponymous town in Aragón in the Longás area, in the north of the province of Zaragoza, which was listed as a contributor to the Monastery of Leire in the year 994, by virtue of its payment of tithes. From Longás, the Lucientes moved to Uncastillo, one of five *villas* with special status in the Zaragoza region. They were *infanzones*, a lower rural nobility title granted from the eleventh century onwards in recognition of and compensation for supporting the Christian monarchy during the conflict, and for supporting the drive to resettle the land.

Goya's maternal ancestor, Juan de Lucientes, was knighted in the name of King Juan II of Aragón by Count Gastón de Foix on 21 May 1466 in Calahorra. Noble families were plentiful in Spain during Goya's time, accounting for 500,000 of a population of just over nine million. In Aragón alone, there were 9000 *hidalgos*.

In the hierarchy of Spanish nobility, a *hidalgo* was considered below a grandee, and other noble titles, and socially inferior to the wealthier knights and outstanding professionals. Their privileges were limited to exemption from most taxes, and their duties included lodging and feeding any royal troops who happened to be passing through.

By the reign of Philip II in 1556, the nobility's golden age was already over. Many, however, were nostalgic for the glory of war and chivalric splendour, and in Goya's day they continued to occupy prominent positions in their towns of residence; they were also given preferential rights over ploughing both common land and that of the local lord, thus expanding the property they owned.

The Lucientes family moved from Uncastillo to Fuendetodos, where they worked as arable and livestock farmers, cultivating their lands and enjoying a comfortable life in a time of economic hardship, disease, and famine. They were actively involved in the town's social life.

Miguel Lucientes, Goya's maternal grandfather and Mayor of Fuendetodos, made over a house in Calle Alhondiga to his pregnant daughter Gracia who lived in Zaragoza, where his grandson Francisco was born on 30 March 1746. Francisco's godmother, Francisca Grasa belonged to one of the five families of *infanzones* in the town, together with the Lucientes, the Aznars, the Jordás and the Salvadors.

Goya's family returned to Zaragoza in 1759 and Francisco remained there until 1775 when, by then a married man, he moved to Madrid. He remained in the Spanish capital until 1824, the year of his exile to the French city of Bordeaux, where he died on 16 April 1828. Later, in 1899, his remains and those of his son's father-in-law, Martín Miguel de Goicoechea, were exhumed and brought to Madrid. He was finally laid to rest in 1919 in the Royal Chapel of St Anthony of La Florida, at the foot of the dome frescos which he himself had painted.

Chapter 4

The Good Life in Aragón's *Campicos*

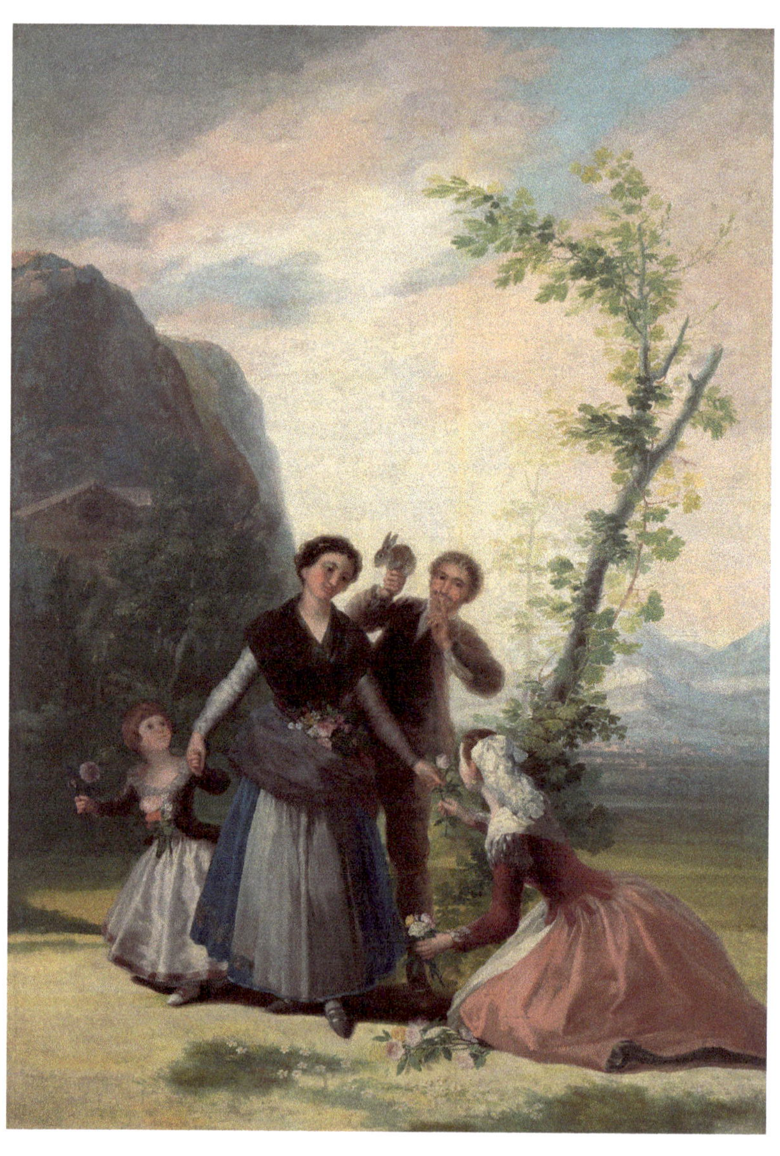

The Flower Girls or Spring.
© Prado Museum Photographic Archive

Neither money, nor the social status acquired as the King's first court painter, nor the bright and ostentatious life and experiences of the older Goya could compare to the calm, wholesome rural and family life of his childhood in Fuendetodos, and he missed it in later life.

Campicos are small, scattered estates of no more than ten hectares like those owned by the Lucientes family in Fuendetodos. They were primarily given over to growing cereal. Yields were adequate for their needs, and they were able to live comfortably from the land, even in those years of scarcity. The Lucientes were *hijosdalgo*, a minor nobility title held by five Fuendetodos families. That, together with their permanent residency, and the office of mayor, held by members of the family at different times, undoubtedly increased the amount of uncultivated land — both communal and owned by the Count of Fuentes — that they were able to plough.

The 1749 land registration process conducted under the auspices of the Marquis of Ensenada sought to establish a single levy, rather than the many that had previously existed, "so that each vassal may pay in proportion to what he has." Scrutiny of the vast data source available reveals much about the activities of farm labourers in Spain at that time. These written records, combined with oral tradition on life in Fuendetodos, the scenes of rural life depicted by Goya, and usage and custom in other Aragonese farming villages give us a good indication of what daily life would have been like for Goya's maternal grandfather, Miguel Lucientes, who had a decisive impact on the artist's memories of his childhood and adolescence.

The records show that the Lucientes had two houses in the village — their main dwelling in the upper part where wealthier farmers lived, and a second in the lower quarter which they gave to their daughter — as well as the Culroya ice pit and a flock of more than a hundred sheep, a shepherd and two pairs of mules. Landowners and farmers, they would probably have owned the equivalent of some seventy *fanegas*[8] and made use of ninety other plots of ploughed land or *roturadas*. Of these, they would have farmed 120 *fanegas* a year, leaving a further forty to lie fallow. The cereal yield would usually have been between ten to one and sixteen to one, bar exceptional years. Probable yields and income have been calculated in the table below.

Yield of the Lucientes family farm. Source: author's own calculations

Crop/ livestock	Area in *fanegas* & live-stock heads	Produc-tion value (*reales de vellón*)	Expenditure (includes daily wages at 4*reales*/ day &inputs)	Gross annual income (*reales*)
Wheat	50	3000	1800	1200
Barley	70	2870	1435	1435
Sheep	100	Annual	Annual	200
Ice pit	Culroya	Annual	Annual	100
Total				2935

The tithes[9] exacted at this point were 10% of 80% of the agricultural output value, minus the 20% accounting for the value of straw. This gives us a total of 2348 *reales*, with tithe payments worth 235 *reales*, making net annual income 2700 *reales*. A net income of this size was far below the 8000 *reales* which a notary or physician would have been earning in Zaragoza at that time, but somewhat higher than the 2400 *reales* paid to a grammar instructor or public attorney and considerably higher than the

---

[8]   One fanega is equivalent to 1.05 hectares
[9]   A tax of 10% of the yield that was paid to the feudal lord.

income of a tailor, master builder or carpenter. This meant the Lucientes were comfortably off both in Fuendetodos and in Zaragoza, where they also had a residence.

In Goya's day, the home of an Aragonese family was not merely to provide shelter for its members, but also a symbol of family dignity. It represented respect and care for parents until their death, it was surety for the rights of the heir and the daughters' dowries when they married, and it provided a home for family members who were either single or experiencing special circumstances.

The rest of this chapter is a novelized description, imagining the daily life of Goya's family, and in particular that of his grandfather Miguel, based on oral and written sources, and the historical memory of Fuendetodos and Aragonese villages of that time.

The spacious house owned by the Lucientes where Grandfather Miguel lived was in the upper part of the village, where the more refined buildings could be found. The more modest house allotted to his daughter Gracia and her husband was — and still is — in Barrio Bajo, at 15, Calle Alhóndiga. This was where the Goyas lived while the paterfamilias José was gilding the altarpieces in the parish church, rebuilt shortly before Goya was born.

Goya's birthplace can still be visited today, now equipped with period furniture and utensils. Built in the seventeenth century, it has a simple masonry façade with three straight, vertically aligned openings and fossil stone blocks on each corner. Its three storeys are connected by a staircase. On the ground floor is the entrance hall and, on the right, a small stable. To the left is a cool room with pitchers and an earthenware jar for water. At the back is a kitchen with a hearth and large fireplace with *cadieras*[10]

---

[10]   Bench for two or three people traditionally placed beside the hearth or fireplace

down the sides. Opposite the hearth is a pantry that leads on to a vegetable garden with a well which can be accessed through a large wooden door.

The first floor is divided into a living room and two bedrooms, while the top floor with its sloping ceilings, houses a 'granary'[11] with wattle and wooden beams, directly under the roof. The granary includes a small room with a hearth to cure the cold meats that were prepared after the pig was slaughtered in the *matanza*, which young Francho[12] used as a space to spend time alone drawing and painting, equipped with pencils, paint-brushes, and sketchbooks. This kept him away from the walls of sheep pens, farm warehouses and other locations he had sometimes bedaubed in the past. The vegetable garden, with its well for watering, grew food for the family. Some produce will have been available all year round, while others, like lettuce, chard, borage, cabbage, watermelon, melon, cucumber, tomato and garlic, were seasonal. Beside the vegetable patch was a fig tree and hackberry. Goya would later recall childhood escapades in the garden with cousins and village friends in pictures like ***Boys Climbing a Tree*** *(Niños trepando a un árbol).*

When the weather was good, the family would take their chairs out into the street in front of their house and gather with their neighbours of an evening. The light of the moon, individual stars or whole constellations would set the stage for their conversations late into the night.

Hens and cockerels roamed the small enclosure beside the garden, supplying eggs all year round, while the sty in the corner by the fig-tree housed a fattened pig, to be slaughtered in November on St Martin's Day. Those who did not breed their

---

[11] This is a rectangular platform used in the construction of roofs, woven with reeds and used to dry fruit

[12] Family nickname for Francisco

own bought a slaughtered pig from the butcher of one of the neighbouring villages and transported it to Fuendetodos on the back of a mule, sometimes coinciding with snowy days like the one Goya depicted in ***The Snowstorm or Winter.***

Every year after supper on St Laurence's Day on 10 August, the Goya brothers would have gone up to the *era* or threshing ground[13] beside their grandfather's house to lie on their backs and watch "Saint Laurence's tears" — as the Perseid meteor shower is known — with its shooting stars speeding across the dark vault of the skies.

After supper once the sun had set, Goya would sometimes have accompanied his parents to the house of their neighbours, the Sánchez family. He might have witnessed them finishing their meal, slurping garlic soup in a wooden bowl from a wooden spoon,[14] a scene he later recalled in one of the Black Paintings at his villa 'Quinta del Sordo' in ***Two Old People Eating Soup*** (*Dos viejos comiendo sopa*).

The young Goya might have felt fearful as he listened to the conversation with the elderly neighbours, sitting on the benches by the hearth, their ancient faces lit up by the glowing embers in intense hues of red and yellow. Their wrinkled faces would have been accentuated in the half-light and their toothless mouths visible as they recounted the old stories of Tosos, fourteen kilometres from Fuendetodos, where witches were said to fly around the eerie Peña Chiquita rock formation, which still guards the entrance to the village. Francisco would have heard the *cierzo* wind howling down the chimney and it may well have recalled the hum of witches like those he painted later in

---

[13]   This is an outdoor area not far from the houses where diverse farm work was carried out like threshing the ears of corn and putting the grain into sacks.

[14]   This was an elderly couple who had moved here from the nearby village of Tosos

Asmodea or Fantastic Vision (*Visión fantástica o Asmodea*) in his Black Paintings in Quinta del Sordo villa. The village witch was said to have used her craft to infect Tosos women with "grimaces and violent movements", making them emulate the gestures of wizards and witches, and causing a violent reaction among the horrified population. In the bottom right corner of his picture, Goya added soldiers firing rifles as if to put an end to the superstitions and impositions of the Old Regime. This period coincided with the French Revolution and the arrival of new ideas that would seek to give ordinary people a more prominent role in resolving their own affairs and finding peaceful solutions to fears such as witchcraft.

When Goya's family left the room on the first floor, they would have used an oil lamp to light their way downstairs. Held aloft, it would have projected distorted silhouettes and giant-sized heads, with Dantesque shadows haunting the whitewashed walls down to the hallway. Such images must have stayed with Francho, who later depicted them in his drawings. Hugh Thomas observed (1979) that these pictures have often been described as a figment of Goya's imagination, whereas many of them might actually reflect his experience of the long winter nights in Aragón.

Goya's grandfather Miguel, with whom the young boy spent much of his time in his early years, managed the Lucientes family farm.[15] The family had farmhands who lived in the village and used a couple of domestic mules and the appropriate tools to undertake more onerous tasks. A servant carried out jobs like bringing up the water from the Old Fountain in pitchers, loaded on their donkey, or taking food to the reapers at harvest time, which was prepared by the women in the house and organized in

---

[15] It would later be taken over by his firstborn heir who was also called Miguel.

the kitchen by grandmother Gracia, the "*dueña*."[16] A neighbour would have helped the Lucientes women with their domestic chores throughout the year.

Apart from the land, Goya's grandfather probably also owned a medium-sized flock of about a hundred sheep and a ram, as well as a buck and a few goats, which would have been taken out to graze by a paid shepherd who lived in a modest dwelling on the same street, Calle de la Alhóndiga. At the end of the road, on the outskirts of the village beside the Old Fountain was the birthing pen where livestock sheltered overnight. Goya recalled the image of the buck in several of his works. Even today dancers dress up in masks and goat's horns at festivals in some Aragonese villages.[17]

Grandfather Miguel would have got up early in the morning before dawn to organize his animals before they were taken out to graze. Breakfast was generally bread soup with garlic, followed by a portion of Aragonese *longaniza* sausage or a salted sardine, with tomato sauce and eaten with a slice of bread from a loaf baked in the village oven, and washed down with red wine drunk from a *porrón* pitcher and made from the garnacha grapes from a local vineyard near Cariñena. The winemaking process is recalled by Goya in **The Grape Harvest or Autumn** (*La Vendimia o El otoño*).

Goya went out hunting with his grandfather for small game like quail, partridge, rabbit, or hare, depending on the time of year. They had two dogs, a pointer, and a chaser, which would have been local mongrels. Their flintlock gun would have been made in the Bustindui workshops in Eibar, with a Spanish-style barrel and beautifully carved walnut stock. Goya would have

---

[16]   'The mistress': this is how the wife of the head of an Aragonese household would have been addressed.

[17]   In a traditional reference to the male goat.

been the *morralero* or porter, carrying the game the grown-ups caught in his backpack.

They would set out from Fuendetodos along the route beside La Casilla pillar, skirted by aromatic thyme, rosemary, sage, and lavender, past the pond and the sheep pen on the hill, which Goya bought for his brother Tomás many years later. As they reached the top of the Great Gorge, the expanse of the Ebro Valley, with its cereal crops, would stretch out for miles in front of them. They might shoot wood pigeons in the pinewoods, or a turtle dove.

As he grew older, Goya went hunting with his uncles Miguel and Juan Esteban on many occasions, first carrying the backpack and, later, firing his first shots. The unforgettable experience turned him into a keen lifelong hunter. They would set traps to catch small birds which they would collect on their way back and put in cages in the little room in the granary in his parents' house. With cousins and friends his own age he set metal traps and wooden sticks covered in glue to trap sparrows. Goya depicted these hunting experiences in drawings and paintings like **Dogs on a Leash** (*Perros en traílla*), **Hunter Loading his Rifle** (*Cazador levantando la escopeta*) and **Hunting with Little Owl** (*Caza con mochuelo*).

Sometimes his grandfather formed a hunting party to chase the bigger game to be found among the rich wildlife that inhabited the gorges and gullies. They would have enjoyed the colourful flora of these limestone ravines carved out by wind and runoff erosion over hundreds of years. Roe deer, wild boar and ibex were some of the species found here. They could also contemplate Egyptian vultures like the one in **Volaverunt** or the owls and other animals which inhabit the etching **The Dream of Reason Produces Monsters**. An excellent display about the ravines, their formation, flora, and fauna can be found at the Asociación Fuendeverde exhibition centre.

In the spring, Grandfather Miguel would have taken delight in the emerald- green plains sown with cereal crops like barley and wheat and splashed with bright red poppies (called *ababol* in Aragonese). By harvest time, they would have changed to gold and then ochre while lying fallow, waiting to be sown again. Strolling around his fields, he would have kept an eye on his farmland to check on the progress of planting, fertilizing and harvesting.

Miguel often paid a visit to the forge and engaged in conversation with the blacksmith and other customers taking ploughshares for sharpening, farm animals to be reshod or simply to comment on the latest news. On other mornings he would converse with the cartwright, and the farmers and drivers waiting for their carts and carriages to be repaired at the workshop.

At cereal harvest time, Goya's grandfather would have supervised the proper stacking of the bundles of hay, which the reapers would tie with esparto rope. Mid-morning, he would take them a fresh wineskin full of wine. The reapers came from outside the village with their own scythes, forming crews which travelled from the south to north of the Iberian Peninsula, following the ripening corn. Their food was cooked at the house of the landowner whose crops they had come to harvest.

On days when the food was particularly delicious and plentiful to help cope with the tough work ahead, Francho would have paid a visit to his grandfather's house where his Aunt Francisca would have prepared him a slice of bread covered with a large slice of ham and accompanied by a few olives pickled in lye and jealously guarded up in the granary in large glass jars covered in water and seasoned with rosemary and thyme.

The corn would have been threshed at Grandfather's threshing ground near the house, using a small wooden platform known as a *trillo* or threshing sled, which was curved at the front and pulled by a mule that circled over the corn spread out on the floor, driven by a person standing or seated on the sled. Goya would sometimes have enjoyed a ride himself, gently pulling the long bridle to make the animal turn. The knapped flint teeth embedded in the bottom of the board released the grain which was then winnowed with four-pronged hayforks.

Once separated from the chaff using a special sieve, the grain was put into three-*fanega* sacks (about 96 kilos) which were then carried on the shoulders up to the attic granary where it was better protected from potential theft. Here the sacks were emptied into a pile which was kept in optimum moisture conditions until it was sold. The straw was collected into semi-spherical haystacks which were covered in mud for better conservation; once the cover was dry, children — like Goya — would climb up and play on the top.

Like most country folk, Grandfather liked to eat early, and the menu usually consisted of a first course of legumes grown in the fields — with a chick pea *cocido* stew on Thursdays — followed by roast lamb or casserole. In hunting season, Sunday lunch would often have been rice with game and snails. A snail basket was kept in the wine storeroom. On other days, partridge was cooked with onions. Seasonal fruit would have been delivered once a week by a fruit seller from nearby Villanueva de Huerva, a so-called "irrigated village" eight kilometres away, and would have included cherries, melon, watermelon, apricots and peaches in spring and summer, grapes and pears in autumn and apples all year round. Wine was cooled in Goya's grandfather's ice pit and drunk from the traditional glass *porrón* pitcher.

The garnacha grapes from a small local vineyard were pressed into the filtering receptacle placed at the mouth of a deep cylindrical vat built under the floor in the room to the right of the entrance hall. Once the juice had fermented into wine, it was stored in small casks in the same room.

Goya's grandfather was also the village mayor, and on Mondays and Thursdays he would go to the town hall, where he and the secretary would attend to any outstanding business and see to the collection of taxes and "first fruits" which, as president of the local board, he was responsible for administering. Of an afternoon, he would play a card game called *guiñote* in the lower part of the inn which had been donated to the village by the Count of Fuentes. It also served as a bar, and he usually won his drinks. He would then go round joining the conversations of the local residents, gathered at the entrances to their homes around domestic activities like shelling almonds, pickling vegetables or sampling the first cold meats made from the slaughtered pig, like *tortetas*[18] or slices of grilled bacon. Then there was the treading of the grapes in the vat to release the juice, and visits paid to acquaintances to pass the time of day over a glass of wine.

At other times, he would walk around the village, past the lavender, and hear women's voices and laughter as he approached the old pond where the horses were watered and is now home to ducks and white swans. Or he might walk over to the Old Fountain, where women and children would be queuing to fill the pitchers which they would then carry on their heads back to the large earthenware jars in the cool rooms in their homes, like those featured in **Women Carrying Pitchers** (*Las mozas del cántaro*) and **A Woman and Two Children by a Fountain** (*Una mujer y dos niños junto a la Fuente*).

On the way back from his walk, Grandfather Miguel would have found his grandsons playing in the street. They might have

---

[18] Typical dish in the highlands of Aragón, particularly in the area around Graus and Huesca, similar to black pudding and made from pigs' blood, breadcrumbs, flour and lard

been playing on a seesaw, climbing fruit trees in the orchards, or looking for birds' nests, throwing hackberry seeds, or blowing into tubes made from reeds; they might have been leapfrogging, playing *marro* — a game of chase — or taking a dip in the local pond, throwing stones or running after dogs. His granddaughters would be skipping or following a pattern traced on the ground beside one of the village threshing grounds. For tea, the grand-children and their friends would have a slice of bread dipped in wine and covered in sugar or a piece of bread and chocolate. Goya recalled this in paintings like ***Children Playing Leapfrog*** *(Niños jugando a pídola)* and ***The Seesaw*** *(El balancín)*.

Often, at the close of day, Goya would see his grandfather's flock of sheep returning to the pen near the Old Fountain. The sheep bells would jangle as they walked slowly home, tired from their long journey across the hills, and with the buck's head rising above them all, a deeper-sounding bell hanging from his neck and a menacing set of horns. This image, particularly their late return on long summer nights, made an impression on the young Goya and featured —transformed by his imagination — in some of his pictures.

Grandfather Miguel's supper would usually have begun with lettuce or cucumber salad, dressed with salt, vinegar and oil made from the local *empeltre* olives, a pale gold variety with a mild, sweet, and fruity flavour, grown on the family's estate and pressed in an oil mill in Belchite. In 1909, Grande Covián, Professor of Biochemistry at the University of Zaragoza and founder of the Spanish Nutrition Society judged the *empeltre* the best olive variety in the world. For second course, he would have had seasonal vegetables boiled with potatoes or mixed with scrambled eggs and tomato. Dessert would have been a portion of sheep's cheese or a glass of fresh milk from the family flock. After supper in the winter, the family would seek warmth on the benches by the fireside, and the conversation might go on late into the night, for as long as the embers continued to glow.

Grandfather slept in a room just off the living area on the first floor, in a bed with an iron head- and footboard gilded with elegant decorative pinecones and circles. The comfortable mattress, filled with pure new lamb's wool from his own flock, was taken out of its cover for beating every spring. There were two bedside tables and two other pieces of furniture. One was an oak wash-set with a mirror, a white porcelain washbasin and, on a side shelf, a blue and white ceramic water pitcher from the village of Muel, with a handle and spout. The other was a wooden chest of seven drawers, also made from oak, for underwear. The big pine wardrobe, made by the cartwright and varnished dark brown, had three sections for daywear and party outfits.

On Saturdays, Grandfather Miguel would go to the barber's for a shave. Sharp, smooth and with mother-of-pearl handles, the razors used were made in the nearby village of Sástago. On Sundays, he would go to mass where some of his grandsons and other youngsters from the village were altar boys. Goya's brother Camilo was always among them. The priest celebrated mass in Latin at the high altar in front of the main retable, with his back to the parishioners who would have been occupying the seats reserved for each family: the women sat at the front, their heads covered with black mantilla shawls, while the men stood at the back of the nave. Everyone would kneel during the consecration, when the priest would be flanked by two altar boys, holding his chasuble so that it did not drag along the floor during the genuflections that accompanied the moment of elevation and the ringing of handbells. Goya depicted the ceremony in ***The Churching of Women*** (*Misa de parida*). His grandfather's relations with the priest were rather strained. As mayor, Miguel had first had to warn and later report his womanizing behaviour, causing the Franciscan preacher Friar Antonio from the Cariñena monastery to intervene, and leading to a trial at the Court of the Holy Inquisition and a ruling in 1754 which forced the priest out of the village and into confinement in the San Carlos Seminary in Zaragoza. Goya's grandfather had to give evidence at the hearing. He would probably have stayed with his relative Polonia whom he visited on his frequent trips to the city.

The clergyman's unfortunate behaviour was the talk of the town, and this together with similar memories may have contributed to Goya's critical etchings of a clergy who often failed to fulfil their mission of Christian example and ministry. ***Dream of Some Men Who Were Eating Us*** (*Sueño de unos hombres que se nos comían*) is a case in point.

In winter, once the last embers in the hearth had died down, the family would make their way to beds heated by warming pans placed under the sheets. Flickering oil lamps would light their way, lengthening and distorting the human shapes on the walls. At night a complete and restful hush would fall upon Fuendetodos, interrupted only at dawn by the crowing of the cockerel and clatter of the mule drivers as they took carts laden with farming tools out into the fields.

Every year in November, a blind man with a guitar would visit Fuendetodos with his young guide. At dusk, in the Plaza Mayor or Main Square, he would sing popular cordel ballads[19] to the crowd. If the popular Spanish saying often heard in Lower Aragon is to be believed, payment was strictly upfront: "If you want the blind man to sing, first throw your money into the ring!" One of the songs in most demand was *Los calzones y las alforjas*. Goya depicted the scene in the well-known oil on canvas tapestry cartoon, ***The Blind Guitarrist*** (*El ciego y la guitarra*)

---

[19]   The booklets containing them were hung up on a cord at open-air fairs, hence the name.

which hung in the antechamber of the Prince and Princess of Asturias.

At the end of May, a *romería* — still celebrated today — processed up to the Chapel of San Roque, announced by a *diana floreada*, a special kind of reveille. Then, as now, the villagers left together mid morning to make the five-kilometre trek up the path that leads north-east through the Valley of Santa María, with its pine-covered slopes, heading for the Great Gorge and then along the path to the right across the fields and pine woods to the chapel in La Puebla de Albortón. After mass, the participants have lunch and are treated to buns and confectionary by the San Roque Brotherhood. They sing local folk songs known as *jotas* before returning to the village and processing into the church.

Also in May, a *cucaña* was set up in the village. This long tree trunk was cut down by the local youths, driven into the ground and smeared with grease during the August festival. Doughnuts were placed at the top to reward the first person to climb up without slipping down. Goya depicted the scene in his tapestry cartoon *La cucaña* or **Greasy Pole**.

In Carnival season, young men would dress up as *trangas*,[20] wearing animal skins, goat horns and blackened faces, scaring children like Goya who would have watched them dance down the street.

Early on Good Friday, altar boys like Francho would run through the village streets, dressed in white habits with plaited waistbands, announcing the early-morning procession along the Stations of the Cross, and clattering *carraclas* and *matracas* built by the cartwright.[21] This 'Way of the Cross' must indeed

---

[20] A carnival costume where the wearer is covered in a goat fleece with horns attached to the head with rope, teeth made from potato, a mask and a club or thick stick.

[21] Small wooden instruments. The *carracla* is a small wooden rattle that makes a dull, low-pitched sound as a ratchet is moved with a handle.

have felt like a penance when the bitter *cierzo* wind was blowing. It was led by the priest who would stop at each of the fourteen stations to read aloud the appropriate text and say a short prayer, with the congregation joining in popular religious songs on their way back to the church. Black and purple mourning ribbons were hung on the house façades during Holy Week.

The Thursday of Corpus Christi was also an important feast day in Fuendetodos. High mass was attended by almost everyone, starting with the mayor, members of the council and its secretary, and the school headmaster. The priest wore an artisan chasuble made of silk with gold embroidery and said mass in Latin with the help of two altar boys, one of which was Francisco's brother Camilo, after he had taken his first communion. Hymns were sung by a small choir featuring the tenor voice of one of Goya's neighbours. After mass, a procession would file along the main streets of the Barrio Alto and the holy sacrament was displayed in an artisan gold monstrance held by the priest beneath a large canopy carried by four young men chosen by the constable. Following behind in their ceremonial costumes were the children who had taken their first communion the month before.

The balconies lining the streets were decorated with white sheets or tapestries with sacred images and banners, while some houses would set up small altars by the front door, where the priest would stop to say the Lord's Prayer, a Hail Mary and a Glory Be.

At the festival of the village patron, Saint Bartholomew, still celebrated on 24 August, a small band of *dulzainas*, lutes, *guitarricos*, drums and tambourines would tour the streets first thing in the mornings, playing the reveille, and liven up the evenings and night-time dances in the main square. More dancing

---

The *matraca* emits a dry, penetrating sound as the striker moves on a platform.

would follow High Mass in the Church of La Asunción on the saint's feast day, presided over by the mayor and the parish priest. In the *baile de la cinta* — rather like maypole dancing — young men and women would dance in pairs to the strains of a *jota* played by a pipe and drum, spinning multi-coloured ribbons around them. An ensemble of guitars and *bandurrias* — or chordophones — would parade through the streets, stopping in courtyards where a singer would dedicate a *jota* he had composed especially for each of the young women who lived there.

On these feast days, the women would prepare special menus starting with a *chilindrón* chicken broth, and roast kid or lamb with potato. Dessert was seasonal fruit followed by homemade cakes with toasted almonds and sun-dried apricots, washed down with wine that had been aged in a cask kept especially for holidays. Water and red wine were kept cool with ice from the Culroya icehouse owned by the Lucientes. In the afternoon, people would play *pelota* hitting a ball against the wall of a house which served as a court, or games of *barras*, throwing small wooden poles like skittles. There were picnics and hot chocolate parties that would have gone down well with the children. Stilt-walking was another tradition, depicted in Goya's **Stilts** (*Los zancos*), and other games would round off the evening, like the reckless races where young men would run in front of Bulls with flaming balls of tar on their horns. Some of this 'entertainment' was not part of the official programme: goats greased with soap would be released by troublemakers to be won as trophies by anyone able to catch them, stirring up considerable commotion. Goya depicts the lathering of such a goat in ***Wait till you've been anointed*** (*Aguarda que te unten*).

The young men would go to the threshing grounds to pit their skills at *pelota* in tournaments with neighbouring villages like the one depicted in Goya's tapestry cartoon ***The Game of***

Pelota (*El juego de la pelota a pala)*. With its splendid sense of perspective and solid main figures in the style of Velázquez, it evokes Goya's early baroque paintings.

On Christmas Eve, Goya would have gone up to his grandfather's house in the upper part of the village to have dinner with the rest of the family in a large dining room on the first floor. There would have been an oak table, tall chairs and a magnificent two-part wooden dresser made from cherry wood, with two lower cupboards which housed their dark blue porcelain tableware, with its chinoiserie pattern made at the Count of Aranda's pottery factory in Alcora. The dresser would have had a pink marble surface with four small columns to support a cabinet for glassware made in Caspe and used only, like the porcelain, on very special occasions.

The room would have been heated with wood-burning stoves with olive wood for fuel. Cardoons in a white pinenut sauce would have been followed with capon in tomato sauce, and *turrón* almond sweets. After dinner, they would have made their way along snowy streets to Midnight Mass, accompanied by *zambomba* drums and Christmas carols sung by schoolchildren.

As in many other villages which belonged to the former Crown of Aragón, the bells in Fuendetodos church came from French factories. Different sounds and cadences marked both religious and secular events: a rapid peal, followed by three upward notes announced Sunday mass; a continuous ringing marked High Mass to commemorate the patron saint; a bell tolled slowly and solemnly was for the dead; the fire warning was fast and furious, and the bells rang out joyfully to announce special occasions, like the pastoral visit from the Archbishop of Zaragoza in May 1746,the village children's first communion or the celebration of weddings and baptisms. From Maundy Thursday to Holy Saturday, the bells fell silent.

Goya lived in Fuendetodos as an infant and child, and moved to Zaragoza at the age of thirteen, but continued to return on visits with his mother for several years. Grandfather Miguel often went to Zaragoza, travelling by stagecoach, a calash which travelled along the cart track through María de Huerva. It would have taken seven hours to complete the seven-league journey. Regular trips included the farm festival in spring or the need to clinch a deal on the sale of ice from the Culroya ice pit with customers like the Carthusian monks of Aula Dei. Then as now, October marked the celebration of Our Lady of the Pillar, when Miguel would have taken part in the 12 October procession. He also attended some of the famous bullfights on horseback, organized by cavalry armories and brotherhoods, which took place in the market square. He would have been able to view them from the balcony of one of the houses and then enjoy the singing and dancing of *jotas* in the streets in the centre of the village.

At midday, he would have headed for Plaza del Pilar to follow the progress of the new chapel commissioned by Archbishop Añoa and designed by architect Ventura Rodríguez, built with materials including the local fossil stone, before drinking a few glasses of wine from Longares in a small tavern in the San Pablo district, near the Posada de las Almas hostel, where he would bump into other people from Fuendetodos now living in Zaragoza.

After lunch, Goya's grandfather would make his way to the bar near his Zaragoza home, in Plaza del Carbón, where the other customers would always make room for him to join their card games and conversations. These would be employees who worked for the government in Zaragoza, small entrepreneurs and shopkeepers enjoying the quiet life in the village. No money was at stake, but losing was a costly business, as the drinks would be on you and your fellow card-players never chose the cheapest options on the list! On many a warm evening — until he was widowed — Miguel would take a stroll with his wife along the banks of the river Ebro.

A theatre enthusiast, Miguel also liked the one-act farces and popular plays on the stage in Zaragoza, where the main shows would be accompanied by supporting acts where young women performed popular dances called *tiranas* and *seguidillas*, and sang bold, saucy songs in luscious voices to the delight of their audiences, sometimes creating uproar in the playhouse. Every year, at the end of summer, he would order a new outfit — a coat, waistcoat, and breeches — that would be made to measure by one of the Zaragoza's excellent tailors.

After his wife died, Goya's grandfather began to spend more time in Zaragoza, but stayed in touch with Fuendetodos. The memory of the good life in an Aragonese rural village enjoyed by his grandfather, surrounded by decent, like-minded neighbours, with a common interest in getting on with their everyday lives, later led Goya to yearn for his past in letters to his friend Martín Zapater: "But my dear boy, *campicos* are the good life, and nobody will convince me otherwise. All the more so now that I am beginning to have greater and ever more bitter enemies."

Goya himself was only able to enjoy this good country life in his childhood, but he did set up his brother Tomás as a farmer in Fuendetodos in 1778, buying him a house, sheep pen and land. As a result, Tomás was able to see out his days in the same village where the brothers had grown up together. He and two of his daughters, Joaquina and Rafaela, married into other wealthy families, and were able to live what the Roman lyric poet Horace referred to in the first century B.C. as *beatus ille*, a notion Goya too would have learned at school with the Piarists: "Happy the man who, remote from business, cultivates his paternal lands with his own oxen, disengaged from every kind of usury... he shuns both the bar and the proud portals of citizens in power."[22]

Tomás's descendants have been mayors of Fuendetodos on several occasions. One of them attended the tribute to Goya, organized by the painter Ignacio Zuloaga in 1913, when the Lucientes's house was being restored, and appears in the television documentary "Goya naturalista", produced in 1984.

---

[22] From *The Works of Horace*, translated by Christopher Smart.

Chapter 5

In Zaragoza

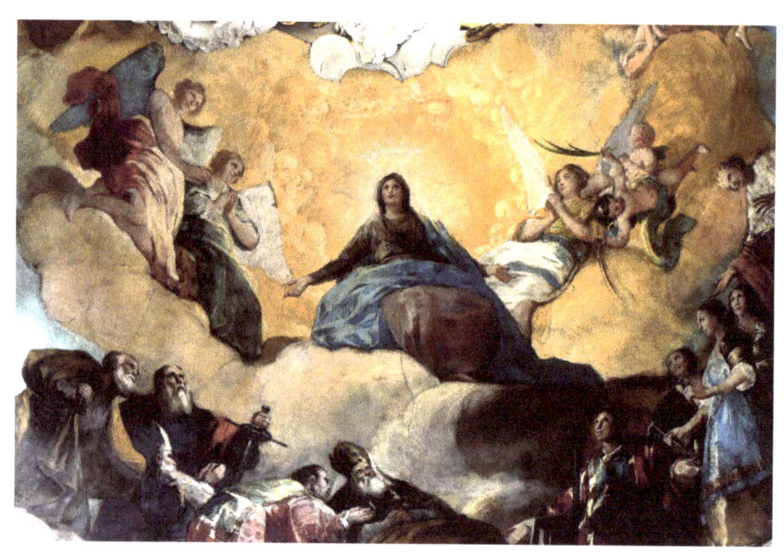

Regina Martyrum Dome of the Cathedral of
Our Lady of the Pillar, Zaragoza, Spain

On 21 May 1736 at the age of twenty-three, Goya's father Joseph married Gracia Lucientes in the Church of San Miguel de los Navarros in Zaragoza. According to the marriage certificate, the wedding ceremony was held in the sacristy, sealing the union of "Joseph Goya, bachelor, gilder by trade, native of this city, son of Pedro and Gertrudis Zúñiga; with Gracia Lucientes, woman, spinster, native of Fuendetodos, son of Miguel and Gracia Salvador, once again resident in this city and members of this parish." The marriage deeds state that the bridegroom was a "journeyman gilder" who had therefore, at this point in time, not yet reached the status of master in his trade.

This was a period when guilds were very important in Zaragoza, both socially and professionally. Becoming a master gilder, as with other trades, required four years as an apprentice, living in the master's house, to first acquire the status of journeyman. A journeyman could then move out of the family home, although he still depended professionally on the master tradesman, and would remain in his workshop until, after the appropriate number of years, he finally obtained the title of master. According to the deeds, when he married, Goya's father was still a journeyman.

The church where the wedding took place was in the same parish where Francho's grandparents lived in Calle del Coso, the family home of their relative Polonia Lucientes. Although they had their own home and land in Fuendetodos, they spent lengthy periods in the city of Zaragoza, which is why the bride, Gracia, appears as a native of Fuendetodos but her parents as "once again resident" in Zaragoza.

Goya's paternal grandfather, Pedro, was a scribe and royal notary, and had bought a house with several adjacent dwellings in Calle de la Morería Cerrada in Zaragoza. Once they married, Goya's parents moved to one of these houses, opposite the Count of Fuentes's palace gardens in what is now Calle Azoque.

In 1745, Gracia became pregnant with Francisco who was born on 30 March 1746, not in Zaragoza, but in Fuendetodos, in a house owned by the Lucientes family, built in the early seventeenth century. Francisco was the third surviving child after Rita and Tomás, who were seven and eight years old respectively when they moved to Fuendetodos. The youngest, Camilo, was born six years after Goya.

The family had moved to Fuendetodos for a number of reasons, which are listed here in greater detail:

1. A drop in his father's income as a gilder due to a reduction in assignments. This was owing to an economic slump in Zaragoza and a policy of removing wood from churches, both because it was a fire hazard and because Enlightenment politicians saw the gilding of altarpieces as excessively costly.

2. The Goyas' house in Calle de la Morería Cerrada in Zaragoza, in the parish of San Gil, was being renovated because it was in a poor state of repair and needed refurbishing for their growing family.

3. Many years of drought and bad harvests had led to severe food shortages in Zaragoza. The city was beset by hunger, riots, diseases like the plague, and terrible sanitary conditions. Two of their children, Jacinta and Mariano, had already died at a young age.

4. Goya's father was assigned the gilding of the magnificent main altarpiece in the parish church of Fuendetodos, which had been painted a few years earlier.

5. Goya's maternal family had substantial farm property in Fuendetodos, making them comfortably off, and Gracia's father offered them a house the family owned in Calle de la Alhóndiga.

6. Their children would have free primary education in the excellent Fuendetodos schools, whereas private schooling in Zaragoza was out of their reach financially.

The history of Goya's family and residence in Zaragoza is very well documented and there are no records of them living in the town between 1746 and 1759 or that their son Francisco went to school there or lived permanently in the city as a boy, although his parents continued to pay taxes and a levy on their house in Calle de la Morería.

In 1750, Goya's father was working on an altarpiece in the Church of Santa Engracia in Zaragoza, and it is known that he lived and worked in the parish of San Miguel, in a house owned by the Virgen de la Sierra Brotherhood, also in Calle del Coso, but that he often travelled to Fuendetodos to be with his family. Although Goya's father was sporadically living and working in Zaragoza, Francisco remained with his mother and siblings in Fuendetodos where he went to school.

The family's ongoing relationship with Zaragoza meant Francisco and his brother were confirmed there in 1751 in the parish church of San Gil, chosen, in line with family tradition, as the church where they had been baptized, like their father, uncles and aunts before them, as had Goya's own brothers and sisters. His younger brother Camilo was also baptized there in 1752.

The move to Zaragoza

In 1759, Goya's family decided to move back to Zaragoza, although they kept their house in Calle de la Alhóndiga in Fuendetodos. They continued to visit, especially in summer, when the children were on school holiday and temperatures were scorching in the capital. At this point, Francisco was 13, his sister Rita 20, older brother Tomás 21 and younger brother Camilo 7. By then, Zaragoza had a population of 43,000, Madrid 156,000, Aragon 600,000 and Spain a total population of ten million.

Professional activities in the city included 3,887 military personnel, as this was a stronghold close to the French border, 2,262 artisans, 1,800 clergy, 1,107 students, 951 farm hands and 744 members of the nobility. The university students were based in twelve colleges, of which seven were religious and five secular institutions.

A dynamic and religious city, Zaragoza was growing both socially and economically. It had many popular festivals and *romerías*, an intense cultural agenda organized primarily by the university and the Enlightenment institution *Sociedad Económica Aragonesa de Amigos del País*, of which Charles III of Spain was later a patron. Like other societies promoted by reformists, its schools taught many different subjects of an eminently practical nature, including Civil Economics and Mathematics — in partnership with the army — Natural History, Development of Popular Industry and Farming. Many major engineering works were underway at this time, including the Imperial Canal, a project run by **Canon Ramón Pignatelli** to bring irrigation to Zaragoza and create fertile land to supply the city with fruit and vegetables. A new bullring was also being built, and the bullfights that took place there featured eminent matadors whom Goya depicted in his paintings and prints.

The aristocracy looked down on manual labour, particularly farm work, and the rural way of life was treated with some contempt. Upper-class families were more concerned with matters of the mind, and spent their time on conversation, courtship, and debating topical matters and issues of every kind in fashionable salons. They gave small concerts and sung opera arias. For them, food was plentiful and select, and included soft drinks and diverse kinds of confectionary and chocolate.

As strong or even stronger than the aspiration for economic well-being was the desire for the social promotion that was so hard to attain and depended on belonging to guilds or high-ranking professions like notaries, physicians, merchants, the clergy, or the military. The guilds formed élite groups set apart from common working people, and membership brought higher social status. Access to these closed associations was limited to the sons and sons-in-law of the affiliated. In the eighteenth century, apart from the pre-requisite entrance exam, membership fees were kept deliberately high to limit the numbers of new confreres. According to the 1723 census, Zaragoza had 133 such guilds, including the gilders, established in 1602, and the painters. Guild stewards presided over processions, parades, and public festivals, which were also an important part of city life. The Corpus Christi procession, held after mass in the cathedral was attended by all the councillors, and finished at the houses by the bridge over the Ebro where *horchata* (tiger nut milk), cinnamon water, sponge cakes, confectionary and chocolate were served. The Feast of the Guardian Angel ended with a string concerto in the Lonja chapel.

Affluent families in Zaragoza frequented an elegant café run by a Neapolitan owner, Carmen Montanino, where, as well as coffee — a recent novelty at the time — they could also enjoy lemonade, barley water or tiger nut milk and a wide variety of sweets and ice cream.

Epidemics were common in Zaragoza and many charitable and medical institutions took in both the physically and mentally ill. The Hospital of Nuestra Señora de Gracia and the Real Casa de la Misericordia provided shelter for beggars and paupers, while the Hospitalico housed boys and girls and educated them to the age of fifteen when they were sent to the master craftsmen's workshops belonging to the guilds. The Monte de Piedad — an institutional pawnbroker run as a charity — helped those in need of loans and offered low-interest credit in exchange for the items held, to prevent the poor and needy from falling into the hands of usurers. The Charitable Board of the *Real Sociedad Económica Aragonesa de Amigos del País* created new jobs for day labourers and other workers who were victims of economic crisis.

The Goyas' return to Zaragoza may have been due to the following circumstances:

1. Goya's father was commissioned for a number of gilding jobs, assisted by his son Tomás who went on to follow in his father's footsteps.
2. The city would offer their children Francisco and Camilo better opportunities to complete their education and start work, Francisco as painter and Camilo in the church.
3. Grandfather Miguel had bestowed a dowry on his daughter Gracia, giving her the Alhóndiga house and some land in Fuendetodos, including ploughing rights. But by this stage, the rules regarding residence in the village and direct cultivation had become more flexible. This meant Goya's mother had a small income of about 500 *reales* a year to help support the family.

The Goya's house in Calle de la Morería was just opposite the palace of the distinguished Pignatelli family, which held the title of Count of Fuentes and Lord of Fuendetodos. Goya probably paid them more than the occasional visit. When, in 1759, he painted the smiling face of an elegantly dressed girl, his model was probably one of the Count's children.

The acquaintance, friendship and respect Goya professed for the Pignatelli family was important throughout his life. He had already met the 16th Count of Fuentes, Juan Joaquín Atanasio Pignatelli de Aragón y Moncayo in Fuendetodos, during one of his yearly visits to sign off his accounts with the council for use of the pinewood and cultivated land he owned there.

In 1741, the Count married María Luisa Gonzaga, daughter of the Duke of Solferino. Goya painted the Italian Jesuit, Saint Aloysius Gonzaga, who was related to the Solferinos in the picture **Saint Aloysius Gonzaga Meditating in his Studio** *(San Luis Gonzaga meditando en su studio)*. The 16th Count was widowed in 1773 and in 1775 married his second wife María de Silva Bazán. Also a widow, she was the mother of Cayetana, the Duchess of Alba, who was just thirteen at that time. Juan Joaquín had seven siblings, with whom Goya was acquainted. These included Vicente, a clergyman and painter, and the driving force behind the drawing school Goya attended, dedicating one of the rooms in his palace for this purpose. He moved to Madrid, where he was a member of the San Fernando Royal Academy of Fine Arts, of which Goya later became director in 1795, after the death of Francisco Bayeu.

Another son, Ramón, became a canon, Enlightenment advocate and sponsor of the Imperial Canal of Aragón. He founded the aforementioned *Real Sociedad Económica Aragonesa de Amigos del País*, ran the Casa de Misericordia hospice, and was rector of the University of Zaragoza. Goya painted **Ramón Pignatelli de Aragón y Moncayo** on one of his visits to Zaragoza when he was already living in Madrid.

José, a Jesuit, was provincial superior of the Society of Jesus and was canonized by Pius XII in 1954 as Saint José de Pignatelli.

The Count's eldest son José María, who married the Count of Aranda's daughter, shared Goya's love of the theatre and his admiration for the beautiful actress María Lavedant. José María died before his father and never inherited the title of count.

It was in 1759 that Goya's family decided to reform the house in La Morería, which they sold in 1760, perhaps because they were unable to pay for the work they had started or because they needed money to complete their children's education. They moved to a series of rented properties in Coso Bajo and Plaza de San Miguel, given the additional complication of needing extra space for Goya's father's workshop.

Goya studied at the Piarist School of Santo Tomás for two years, in the class of Father Joaquín Ibáñez de Jesús María, where he met his classmate *Martín Zapater Clavería*, who would become his friend and confidant for 24 years. Goya wrote 147 letters to his friend between 1775, when he moved to Madrid, and 1799. That Goya spent just a short time at this school appears to be confirmed by his failure to mention any other schoolfellows in his correspondence. Nor does he refer to student escapades, difficulties with schoolwork, grades obtained or any other aspect of his education here. That he was in Father Joaquín's class is corroborated in one of his letters referring to their days together at the Piarists.

The Piarists or Escolapios, as they were known in Zaragoza, cared about their pupils' education and the school had excellent teachers, like humanist Father Basilio Boggiero, who taught rhetoric. He was a friend of Palafox and later a hero of the Zaragoza Sieges, during which he was shot by the French in 1809. In his book of poems published in 1817, he refers to Goya in the prologue as "the famous painter." Piarist schools were also well known for a unique approach to handwriting, with elegant, tall, and thick but simple characters — the origin of Goya's own writing style.

The Piarist church and school building, which still exist today, opened in 1740. The Piarists were held in great esteem in Zaragoza because they treated their pupils well and their teachers were highly knowledgeable on subjects ranging from pronunciation, writing and numeracy to Christian doctrine. They often organized events where pupils could display their knowledge of the various subjects they studied, including literature and rhetoric, poetry, and catechism.

In 1819, Goya was commissioned to paint the Prior of the Church of Saint Anton in Madrid, giving rise to the sublimely mystic ***Last Communion of Saint Joseph Calasanz*** (*Última comunión de San José de Calasanz*) founder of the Piarists or Escolapios, buried in the Church of Saint Pantaleo in Rome.

Goya was already familiar with Zaragoza and integrated quickly in its social life. His father already had a house in the city, which he had often used on previous occasions, such as his own and his brothers' confirmations, or when his younger brother was baptized. The year the family returned to the city was also the year Ferdinand VI of Spain died and was succeeded by his half-brother Charles III. The third son of Philip V and Elisabeth Farnese, Charles was already King of the Two Sicilies (Naples and Sicily) when he became King of Spain. Born in Madrid in 1716, Charles had been Duke of Parma through his mother's side from 1731 to 1735. The Kingdom of the Two Sicilies had belonged to the Crown of Aragón since the thirteenth century but was lost to Spain in the treaties derived from the War of the Spanish Succession (1701-1714) which recognized Philip V as King of Spain. Philip wished to recover it and entrusted the fight against the Austrians to his son Charles. The Spanish and French troops, led by Captain General José Carrillo de Albornoz defeated the Austrians at the Battle of Bitonto in 1734, and Charles was crowned King of the Two Sicilies.

Carrillo de Albornoz was appointed Viceroy of Sicily and Grandee of Spain, under the title Duke of Montemar. His remains were laid to rest in the mausoleum of the Chapel of Saint Joachim in the Basilica of El Pilar in 1766. Goya was therefore resident in Zaragoza in October 1759, when the new King Charles III stopped over for a month, with his wife Maria Amalia of Saxony and the Prince of Asturias Carlos Antonio, on his way from Naples to Madrid.

The King was met with great pomp and circumstance, beginning with his entrance into the city in a splendidly decorated carriage, escorted by four horsemen in full-dress uniform, followed by three horse-drawn coaches and preceded by two companies of regiments of the grenadiers of Aragón and Zaragoza, each with their own marching band. The glovers' guild paraded with a group of Moors. An infantry regiment brought up the rear of the procession and different trade guilds raised arches of flowers and monuments en route to the palace of the *Real Audiencia* (law court), in Calle del Coso, built in 1552 by the Viceroy of Aragón — then the Count of Luna — which still retains its magnificent semi-circular arch flanked by two colossuses hoisting cudgels. In the evening a "fire machine" — a special figure built for the occasion — was burned in El Coso, opposite the playhouse, and fireworks were lit on the banks of the Ebro.

During his stay, the King went hunting in the Torrero hills and received a request from Aragón's leading politician, the Count of Aranda, to continue work on the Imperial Canal which had previously obtained royal approval and was now being directed by Ramón Pignatelli, at this time Canon at the Basilica of El Pilar. The canal was completed in 1790, producing one of the most fertile and extensive plains in Spain, allowing for the irrigation of 26,000 hectares in Aragón and Navarra. The King was well acquainted with the Count of Aranda who had served him in the war against the Austrians in a bid to recover the Kingdom of the Two Sicilies and was seriously wounded in battle.

Work on the canal was also promoted by enlightened Secretary of State, the **Count of Floridablanca** (*El conde de Floridablanca)*, who drummed up funding both at home and abroad, and was painted by Goya on two occasions. The artist painted himself into one of these portraits, in a stance of virtual genuflection before the Count's imposing figure which is surrounded by drawings of the Imperial Canal.

The right to use the waters of the river Ebro for irrigation purposes was first awarded by Alfonso I, known as The Battler, in 1125, to the Irrigation Brotherhoods. In 1528, after the Monzón Courts, Carlos V agreed to the project designed by Gil Morlanes which established the site of the dam from which the water would be diverted to what would be called the Imperial Canal in El Bocal, near Fontellas: but the work only actually reached the village of Garrapinillos.

No further progress was made until 1772 when the huge financial and engineering undertaking was promoted by the Count of Aranda and approved by Charles III, who then appointed Ramón de Pignatelli to take care of the project. Many major experts of the day were involved in its construction, including works inspector Agustín de Betancourt, a Canary Islander who put into practice the knowledge of hydraulics he had obtained on his trips abroad. Founder of the Spanish School of Civil Engineers, de Betancourt also undertook many major works in Russia for Tsar Alexander I in the last sixteen years of his life.

In 1774, the canal's waters reached Fuente de los Incrédulos, in Zaragoza, where the following inscription can be seen "Incredulorum covictioni et viatorum commodo, 1786" (To make this known to the incredulous and offer rest to the traveller).

So impressed was Goya by the ostentation surrounding the new king and his court, that two burning desires were engraved upon him, both of which he was later able to realise: to visit Naples and to meet Charles III in person to paint his portrait. The result was **Charles III in Hunting Dress** *(Carlos III, cazador)*, a reminder of the monarch's passion for hunting.

In 1759, Goya also attended Grammar classes with the Jesuits whose exclusive rights over the subject meant it could not be taught by the Piarists. The classes took place in public schools known as *aulas reales*, and were given by José Pignatelli, who also taught catechism in the poor neighbourhoods of Zaragoza.

Goya, according to his son Javier, also "studied drawing from the age of thirteen at the Zaragoza Academy of Drawing under the direction of José Luzán." It was in this academy in Calle Platería, which the Junta Preparatoria (board) had established in 1754 where Goya learned the principles of this art. He attended the academy at six o'clock every evening to copy coloured vignettes of works by foreign artists and draw parts of the human body, with special attention to hands and faces, which he later went on to use in his portraits, perfecting and mastering the drawing of lines and curves. Geometry and perspective were also studied as training methods. As an apprentice, Goya helped Luzán prepare his commissions. He would have had to grind up colour powders, mount canvases, prepare primers and varnish the finished paintings.

José Luzán y Martínez, who was friends with Goya's father, had been a court painter and taught in Naples from 1730 to 1736. In his classes, he used the print collection he had brought from his visit to Italy, which included French and Italian Baroque classicists and Rococo style, which influenced Goya's first works

Saint Joseph's Dream (*El sueño de San José)* and ***The Burial of Christ*** (*El entierro de Cristo).* The drawings of major Italian sixteenth-century artists made available by Vicente de Pignatelli, brother of the Count of Fuentes, also served as models for his pictures. In Luzán's classes, Goya met other apprentices who later went on to become major painters and sculptors.

At the drawing academy, Goya was not the typical young apprentice from the villages who lived at the master's house, but the son of a master gilder — albeit one without much work — who knew Luzán's family. With his characteristic empathy and noble nature, he became friends with classmates like the three Bayeu brothers, from the well-known family of Zaragozan painters who would later become his brothers-in-law. Francisco and Ramón were later court painters, while younger brother Manuel became a friar at the Aula Dei Charterhouse, as well as an outstanding painter. Francisco Bayeu taught at the drawing academy before attaining his position at court, following the Late Baroque Italian style of Corrado Giaquinto and later a progressive Classicism.

Goya also befriended Martín Miguel Goicoechea, who came from a wealthy bourgeois family, and would later become his son's father-in-law. The mortal remains of both now lie in the Royal Chapel of Saint Anthony of La Florida in Madrid.

When the family moved to Zaragoza, Goya's brother Tomás assisted his father as a gilder, while sister Rita took care of domestic chores with her mother, and Camilo began his lengthy training to become a priest. After reading and writing, he would have moved on to humanities, four years of art followed by ten of philosophy and moral theology. He received his first tonsure at the age of 24 and was appointed Chaplain of Chinchón, at the age of 32, on a recommendation from his brother Francisco who was in the process of painting the portrait of the Infante Don Luis, Lord of Chinchón in 1784. In 1808, while Camilo was still Chaplain of Chinchón, French troops pillaged and burned the art works in the church. In response, in 1812, Goya painted the beautiful picture ***The Assumption of the Virgin Mary*** *(Asunción de Nuestra Señora)* for the high altar of the parish church.

There is an abundance of work painted by Goya while living in Zaragoza. The next section covers some of the more significant examples and the relevant events in his life with which they coincided.

In this early period, Goya painted small compositions on different subjects: ***Village path*** (*Camino del pueblo*), ***Village Street*** (*Una calle de pueblo*) and ***Night Procession with the Holy Sacrament*** (*Procesión nocturna con el Santísimo Sacramento*). Although the last of these is attributed to him, its whereabouts is unknown, leaving only a photograph of a group of priests carrying a monstrance in the middle of a dark street. Other works include ***Boy with a Bindle*** *(El chico del capazo)*, which depicts a young farm worker or "*chulo*" in popular dress and ***Little Blonde Girl*** (*La niña rubia*). This is the delightful little girl Goya had seen in the palace of the Count of Fuentes near his parents' house, and whose kindly face also reappears in later works, such as those of ***The Duke and Duchess of Osuna and Their Children*** (*Familia del duque de Osuna*).

In 1764, Goya's maternal aunt Francisca and relative Francisco Lucientes were sent to the mental health institution in Zaragoza known as Hospital Real y General de Nuestra Señora de Gracia. Goya's knowledge of this hospital and its patients were reflected in a number of his works, including ***Yard with Lunatics*** (*Corral de locos).*

As a teenager and youth, Goya is said to have been rowdy and argumentative, and was consequently no stranger to brawls between different neighbourhoods and brotherhoods. Of particular significance was the fight that year during the processions of ***The Dawn Rosary*** (*Rosario de la Aurora*) between confreres of the parishes of San Pablo and La Magdalena. Goaded by violent criminals who haunted the streets at night, neither of the two brotherhoods wished to give way to the other in the darkness of a narrow lane and began fighting with lanterns and flagpoles. This is the origin of the Spanish expression "to finish like the Dawn Rosary" to describe events where everything ends in turmoil and confusion. Several were injured and three young men died from knife wounds, leading Goya, who had also been involved — at least according to his biographers in the Romantic period — to leave Zaragoza and take refuge in Madrid. Other accounts claim Goya left for Calatayud, where he decorated the pendentives of the dome in the Jesuit church known today as San Juan el Real.

The eighteenth century saw many serious riots in major Spanish cities, primarily because of a shortage of food and the liberalization of the price of bread. In Madrid, these were known as the Esquilache Riots in March 1766, and were motivated both by hunger and by measures introduced by Charles III's minister the Marqués de Esquilache, prohibiting the use of the traditional garment of a long cape and broad-brimmed hat. One of the consequences of the riots was the expulsion of the Jesuits from Spain. In Zaragoza, in early April 1766, the popular uprising against the price and lack of bread, oil and other staple goods and demanding an improvement in the terrible sanitary conditions was known as the Bread Riot or Broqueleros. *Broquels* were the sets of small shields and weapons with which the riot was brutally suppressed resulting in great bloodshed. The Jesuit priest José de Pignatelli acted as peacemaker during these disturbances.

Also in 1766, Francisco Bayeu was summoned to Madrid by Mengs to become part of his team and appointed first court painter and director of the San Fernando Royal Academy of Fine Arts. He was on the jury of the 1766 painting competition, in which the gold medal was awarded to the excellent painting of his brother Ramón Bayeu, rather than the picture submitted by Goya.

Goya left Zaragoza for Italy between late 1770 and June 1771. He travelled by land via Piamonte, visiting cities en route including Milan, Parma, Padua, Venice, Ferrara, Bologna, and Ancona, until he reached Rome, according to notes in what is known as his Italian Sketchbook. He spent over a month in Rome before sailing home via Civitavecchia and Genoa.

When he later presented his curriculum to become court painter, he claimed to have painted in Rome where "he managed and existed at his own expense."

The ambassador in Rome at that time was from Zaragoza, like Goya. Tomás de Azpuru y Ximénez had been the archpriest of Belchite, in the Chapter of Zaragoza, and was an auditor at the Tribunal of the Roman Rota on behalf of the kingdoms of the Crown of Aragón. Manuel de Prada y Arrieta, also from Zaragoza, was plenipotentiary minister of Spain to the Holy See. He was appointed Archbishop of Valencia in 1770, and Goya attended his ordination ceremony.

Another native of Aragon was the cultivated and enlightened José Nicolás de Azara, the publisher of Virgil's works and the King's agent and procurator general at the Court of Parma. It was he who advised Goya to enter Parma's painting competition, having sent him a picture on the theme of Hannibal with the motto taken from Virgil's Aeneid, "And finally we reach the elusive coasts of Italy."

José Nicolás was a great friend and biographer of Mengs, whom he described as a philosopher who painted for philosophers. Mengs painted his portrait in 1774. Later, when Mengs was court painter in Madrid, he took first Bayeu, who was living in Zaragoza, to work with him, and then Goya, whom he hired to paint tapestry cartoons for the Royal Tapestry Factory he directed. José Nicolás was the brother of the eminent naturalist **Félix de Azara**, who was born in a small village in Huesca called Barbuñales, and who Goya subsequently painted in 1805, in one of his best portraits.

Goya followed Azara's advice and presented ***The Victorious Hannibal Seeing Italy from the Alps for the First Time*** (*Aníbal, vencedor, que desde lo alto de los Alpes, contempla por primera vez Italia)*, winning second prize.

The Duchy of Parma, which belonged to the Crown of Aragón, was governed by the Bourbon Duke, Ferdinand I of Parma, the grandson of both Philip V, King of Spain and Louis XV, King of France, and Spanish could often be heard on its streets.

It is highly likely that during this trip, Goya visited José de Pignatelli in Naples, Bologna, or Ferrara, as the Spanish priest had been living in Italy since the Jesuits were expelled from Spain, and he was the Society's provincial superior in Italy, at the time under the protection of the orthodox Tsarina Catherine of Russia. Pignatelli introduced Goya to a member of the Russian court and suggested him as the Empress's court painter.

However, his father's illness led Goya to return from Italy to Zaragoza. His father stopped working as a gilder the same year, although he continued to carry out inspections on works like the grille in front of the Holy Chapel housing the venerated image of the Virgin of the Pilar. Goya's son Javier referred to the "blind affection he always showed his parents which led him to return home more promptly." On his return from Rome to Zaragoza, in June-July 1771, he set up a workshop in Arco de la Nao, near El Coso and Plaza de San Miguel. In the same year, he painted his first portrait dedicated to Coronel **Manuel Vargas Machuca**, whose family came from Aragón and had settled in Naples. On 21 October 1771, the Basilica's works board — comprising 350 representatives from different levels of society — and the Chapter administrator, proposed that Goya paint the fresco in the dome of the small choir, the *coreto*, opposite the Holy Chapel. The proposal was accepted and brought before the Chapter which approved the project for the sum of 15,000 *reales*, leading to the elimination of the other candidate, Antonio González Velázquez, who had set a higher price. Goya presented his drawing for the fresco on the theme of the ***Adoration of the Name of God*** or ***The Glory*** (*La adoración del nombre de Dios o La Gloria*) which he painted in 1772. The architect of the Basilica choir was Ventura Rodríguez, a friend of Juan Martín de Goicoechea and Martín Zapater. This marked the magnificent start of Goya's mural paintings, in a prototype Baroque style, quite removed from Neoclassicism, to which he would return in works like the other frescos in the Basilica and in the Royal Chapel of Saint Anthony of La Florida.

Also in 1772, he painted two small pictures of ***Worshippers at the Foot of a Cross*** (*Devotos a los pies de una cruz*) following Bayeu's style and ***Saint Fidelis of Sigmaringen*** (*San Fidel de Sigmaringen*) perfectly executed in dark tones. In the same year, he painted the walls of the oratory in the palace of the Count of Sobradiel, Joaquín Cayetano Cavero, on Plaza del Justicia en Zaragoza, which were later transferred to canvas.

Recalling these years as a single man in Zaragoza, Goya later went on to paint subjects far removed from religious themes, depicting moments of leisure like picnics, drinking wine, and laughing with friends, as in ***The Lame Man of Remolinos Opening the Hatches to Put More in. Poor Ramona!***

On 25 July 1773, at the age of 27, Goya married María Josefa Bayeu, aged 26, sister of his painter friends from the José Luzán's workshop. Josefa was related to the Lucientes, as her first cousin Joseph Bayeu was married to Valera Lucientes, Goya's aunt. The wedding took place at the Church of Saint Martin in Madrid, and the couple moved to an elegant house in El Coso district of Zaragoza known as "House of the Dogs", where Goya painted his First ***Self-Portrait.*** Announcing a romantic style, his face is brightly lit against the dark background, his hair loose and his gaze profound. Also in 1773, he painted ***Saint Barbara***, based on a drawing from his Italian Sketchbook which would later serve as a model for the paintings in the Aula Dei Charterhouse.

Goya and Josefa lived together for forty years until her death in 1812. During this lengthy period, Josefa became pregnant twenty times and gave birth to eight children, of which only Javier survived. He drew her portrait seated, in profile, in an etching in 1805, when she was 58. Looking tired and aged, she is wearing a simple but elegant gauze headdress with ribbons and bows.

Goya remained in Zaragoza for sixteen years until 1775 when he moved to Madrid, at the age of 29. First, he and his wife and son Javier lived with the Bayeus in Josefa's family home, at numbers 7 and 9, Calle del Reloj. In 1779, they moved to 1, Calle del Desengaño, where they took in Goya's mother and sister for a year after the death of his father, until Gracia and her daughter went to live with Goya's brother Camilo in Chinchón. Goya also hosted Tomás and his family while his brother was doing gilding work in Madrid.

By way of letter of presentation in Madrid, his mother had noted the family Lucientes' claims to nobility, awarded by King John II of Aragón, their connections with the nobility in Uncastillo and their status as *hidalgos* in Fuendetodos, alongside a list of people to visit. This maternal desire to vouch for her son's aristocratic roots and to enhance her son's grandeur must have been an important aspect in the development of Goya's sense of self and would lead him to aspire to a title later in life, albeit one based on those of ancestors on his father's side, who bore the name Goya, rather than those of his mother.

The first commissions assigned to him that year in Madrid were tapestry cartoons on hunting themes, of which he himself had experience both in Fuendetodos and Zaragoza, and in which he reflected natural life in the region of Aragón where he had grown up.

In 1780, commissioned by the Chapter of the Basilica of El Pilar, Goya returned briefly to Zaragoza to paint the vault beside the Holy Chapel with the fresco ***Regina Martyrum*** and its four pendentives, featuring the four virtues Faith, Fortitude, Patience, and Charity. Both the Chapter and Goya's brother-in-law Francisco — the Basilica's director of painting — criticized the sketches, which subsequently had to be corrected, leading to professional enmity between the two men and tainting Goya's memory of Zaragoza. José, Goya's father, died in 1781 in the house where they were living at the time in Calle Rufas. He was buried in the same church in which he had married Goya's mother, San Miguel de los Navarros. José died intestate because "he had nothing to bequeath", and yet he left four children, one of whom would become one of the world's greatest painters.

When José Goya died, at the age of 68, his wife Gracia was 65, and his children Tomás 42, Rita 44, Francisco 35, and Camilo 29. The family income came primarily from Goya's work as a painter, as Tomás's gilding work tended to be sporadic and was not large scale, while Camilo was still a student. The small amount of land Gracia had received as a dowry had since been sold. Goya took charge of his family and always supported his mother and siblings. He managed to find Tomás work gilding the frames of his paintings for the Aula Dei Charterhouse, and at the palace of the Count of Sobradiel while he was painting the oratory frescos, as well as in several churches in Madrid between 1787 and 1789. Once he moved to Madrid himself, Goya constantly sent back money to his family via his friend Martín Zapater. He recommended his brother Camilo for the post of chaplain at the collegiate church in Chinchón, where his mother Gracia later died.

Visit to Zaragoza in 1808

The French Republican General Napoleon Bonaparte was crowned Emperor of France on 18 May 1804, and King of Italy in 1805. The Franco-Spanish fleet was defeated by the British in Trafalgar on 21 October 1805. One of the consequences was the European commercial blockade Napoleon decreed against Britain, which Portugal failed to respect. Napoleon signed a pact with Charles IV's prime minister Manuel Godoy for his army to pass through Spain to take Portugal, but Napoleon ultimately used this excuse to deploy French troops all across Spain, which he subsequently occupied.

In Madrid, on 2 May 1808, the Spanish people revolted against the French invaders and in the Puerta del Sol a squadron of the dreaded Mameluke cavalry regiment was knifed to death by the people of Madrid who then continued the fight in the streets. On 3 May, the French army bloodily repressed the *madrileños* and executed many citizens. Both events were depicted by Goya in his impressive ***The Second of May 1808 in Madrid*** (*Dos de mayo de 1808 en Madrid*) and ***The Third of May 1808 in Madrid*** (*Tres de mayo de 1808 en Madrid*).

Goya returned to Zaragoza in October 1808, at the request of General Palafox, who called on him to provide testimony of the terrible war against the French. The scenes he witnessed, and the brutality and devastation Aragón and its people had suffered, especially in Zaragoza, featured in many of his works. Goya arrived after the first siege and hastily drew two sketches of the main ruins and disasters, one of which depicts boys dragging the bodies of French soldiers down Calle del Coso. His visit is not evidence that Goya actually witnessed events like the one shown in the print **What Courage!** (¡*Que valor!),* recounting the heroism of Agustina of Aragón, from the hamlet of Fulleda in Lérida, but are certainly the inspiration for later drawings of the Sieges of Zaragoza and their terrible consequences.

By the end of November, Napoleon's troops were once again approaching Zaragoza, curtailing Goya's chance to depict these disasters of war, and afraid that the French might see the sketches he had made, he departed for Fuendetodos, covering his work with paint wash to hide it. Forty-nine years had elapsed since he had left his home village as a boy, and this final trip was to revive many early memories.

The Sieges have given rise to a wealth of historiography and artistic expression in the form of drawing, painting, drama, poetry, musical compositions, and films, perhaps none quite as well known as ***The Disasters of War*** etching series.

When the Spanish General Espoz y Mina recovered the city of Zaragoza in 1813, its population had fallen from fifty to twenty-five thousand.

Goya often mentions Zaragoza both in his letters to Zapater and in many of his works. The city was always close to his heart as the following list of references suggests.

- When he moved from Zaragoza to Madrid in 1775, he wrote in his Italian Sketchbook: *"Zaaragoza, Corazón, Zargoza, Zaragoza* [sic]."
- In a letter to Zapater of 1787, he writes: "What could be more pleasing to me than to go to Zaragoza for a couple of months and live with you and Goicoechea."
- In a letter dated March 1793, he thanks Zapater for sending oil and writes: "I very much appreciate the *pellejito* (animal skin used to hold the wine or oil) and I would appreciate it even more if that were an Aragonese word rather than a Castilian one."
- In his signature on Saints Justa and Rufina, painted for Seville Cathedral, he adds "Augustine Caesar" in memory of the founder of Zaragoza, the Roman emperor Caesar Augustus.
- In his ***Self portrait of 1815***, he signed himself "Fr. Goya aragonés" (Francisco Goya of Aragón).

When appointed a distinguished member of the Royal Academy of Noble and Fine Arts of San Luis in Zaragoza in 1796, he wrote:

> "Of the many circumstances that cause me to appreciate this gift all the more deeply, the first is the origin of so esteemed and respectable a body which ennobles the Homeland I love and of which I am proud to be a son."

Chapter 6

Goya in Society

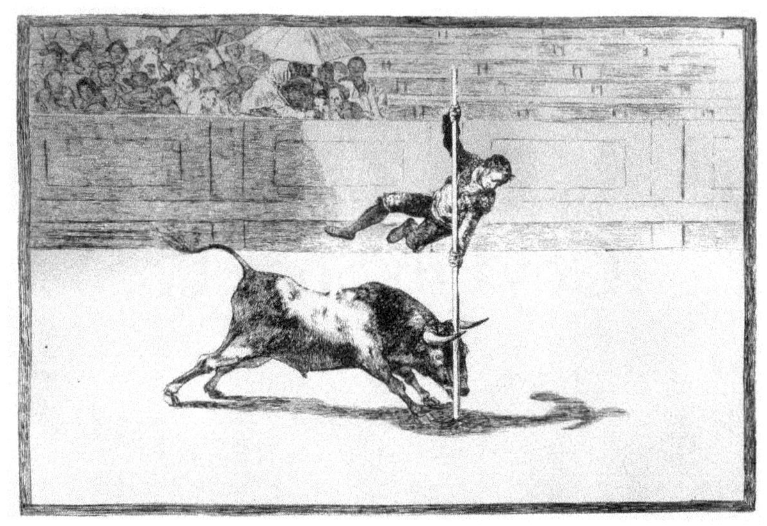

*The Agility and Audacity of Juanito Apiñani
in the Ring at Madrid.*
© Prado Museum Photographic Archive

After his arrival from Fuendetodos in 1759, at the age of thirteen, Goya remained in Zaragoza[23] until he moved to Madrid, a married man, in 1775, when he was 29. These 16 years coincided with his adolescence and early youth, a time which, for Jean Piaget (1966), as mentioned earlier, marks the end of the formal operational stage and the sequence of cognitive development. It's at these stages when the self and personal identity are asserted, and major changes take place in perceptions of bodily image, sexual behaviour, self-esteem, in the social and moral fields, and in friendship. It is also a moment for rebellion against adults and prevailing norms.

Zaragoza had been the capital of the Kingdom of Aragón and was a major city, with a population close to 50,000. It was a hive of activity, in which Goya soon became involved, which greatly influenced his character development. While living in Zaragoza, he enjoyed many of the pastimes typical of the daily life of its inhabitants. Below we consider some of the activities that were particularly important for Goya.

Bullfighting

Goya was a great bullfighting enthusiast and proud of it, as he revealed in his letters to school friend Martín Zapater, which he signed "From Francisco of the Bulls." His passion for what in Spain is often as "*la fiesta nacional*" (the national pastime) began when he was a young man attending amateur *capeas* and continued in Madrid where he depicted it in his bullfighting series. As an old man in exile in Bordeaux, he dedicated his time and art to a series of four exquisite lithographs, ***The Bulls of Bordeaux***.

---

[23] This chapter primarily draws on information in the Government of Aragón's publication issued to mark the 250th anniversary of Goya's birth, in 1996, which covers the lectures that were organised by the Centenary Board.

In a letter written in Bordeaux, Leandro Fernández Moratín notes that "Goya claims he was once a bullfighter and that, rapier in hand, he fears no one, even though he will be eighty in two months' time." In Zaragoza, Goya befriended *novilleros* and bullfighters, who, seeing his fiery temperament and decisive character, sometimes let him take part in capeas held in neighbouring villages which went on late into the night, washed down with wine and liquor, and accompanied by popular performers who danced and sang to the strains of guitars. His friend Martín Zapater sometimes accompanied him on these escapades, as Goya reminded him in one of his letters: "You and I were such rogues."

Goya's first contemporary biographer, Valentín Carderera was also a bullfighting enthusiast and discovered what is thought to be a self-portrait of the artist in the tapestry cartoon **Amateur Bullfight** (*La novillada*) where Goya can be seen fighting a bullock with an amused look on his face as he turns towards his audience. Carderera also notes that Goya was a different man on bullfighting days, "with his big hat, jacket and three-quarter length cape, and his sword under his arm, he engages with the most acclaimed bullfighters...identifying the innermost part of their character as heroes." Many of these bullfighters would dedicate their fights to him.

Bullfighting was an ancient tradition in Zaragoza. By 1328, there were already royal bull festivals in the court of the Aljafería Palace in honour of the newly crowned Alfonso IV of Aragón. Later, in 1790, it was decreed that no licence was necessary to hold "running with heifers and bullocks."

In his early youth, Goya witnessed the crude reality and power of bloody bullfights where rash men, bull fighters and *picadores* on horseback, confronted bulls, injuring them badly on any part of their bodies, piercing them with swords and pikes, and setting dogs on them — as seen in **Dogs on the Bull** (*Perros al toro*) — to enrage the animal when it was deemed too docile. If the bull remained immobile, assistants — usually Moors — hacked it with their crescent-shaped swords, as Goya depicted in **Approaching the bull with lances, scimitars, banderillas and other weapons** (*Desjarrete de la canalla con lanzas, medias-lunas, banderillas y otras armas*). It was a genuine massacre, to whose cruelty Cadalso — a bullfighting opponent — attested before his death in 1782, stating that Spaniards paid money "to watch blood being shed and consider this to be entertainment." Other authors, like Jean-Jacques Rousseau viewed bullfighting as contributing to "preserve the valour of the Spanish people."

To lighten the tension, bullfights were accompanied by shows of a more festive kind, including farce and more light-hearted comical acts. There were performances by "La Pajuelera", a woman who wore a picador's suit and sat astride a pony to pierce huge bulls; Ramón de la Rosa was a black man who would sing to a guitar seated on a bullock; clownish figures would ride on each other's backs, jabbing at the bull with a lance.

On his return from Italy, Goya noted a substantial change in bullfighting practice. Plasticity and aesthetics had begun to play a key role and the matador's skill and art in controlling the bull's strength came to prevail. Bullfighters were professional and popular figures whose performances were attended by beautiful women who vied for a place on the best balconies, both to see and be seen, as Goya depicted in **Majas on a Balcony** (*Majas al balcón*).

On 9 October 1764, Goya attended the opening of the bullring of the *Casa de la Misericordia*, built on the initiative of Canon Ramón de Pignatelli. The splendid ring, with capacity for 8000 spectators, was as impressive as the one in Madrid. Fights would include up to 16 bulls, and the famous Aragonese bullfighter Martincho was one of those who performed there. The many shows held every year to celebrate local and national feast days and special royal occasions featured some of the best-known figures of the day.

It was these leading figures in the world of bullfighting who laid down some of the early rules of the art. Joaquín Rodríguez, also known as *"Costillares"*, invented the *volapié,* a wounding thrust which involved approaching the bull if the animal failed to charge, and piercing it with the sword with a rapid foot movement where his feet appeared to fly, taking him safely away from the bull's horns. He also introduced the order in which the different members of the team performed and assisted in the ring, as well as designing a new outfit, with the silk sash, sleek hairnet and short, decorated bolero jacket that are now so famous. Goya painted a half-length portrait of an elegant Costillares with a bow tie and a kerchief on his head to pin back his hair.

Goya painted nine portraits of the bullfighters he met and saw perform, first in Zaragoza and then in Madrid. He portrayed his favourite, **Pedro Romero** from Ronda, on no less than four occasions, in a tribute to his magnificent art and style. Romero studied each bull before he fought it to fine-tune his technique, dominating the animal by leading it slowly and gently with his cape, before completing the *volapié* boldly and effectively. Goya also painted his brother José Romero in a magnificent portrait in the costume given to him by the Duchess of Alba.

José Delgado, also known as Pepe Illo, introduced ornamental movements and new ways of casting the cape, one of which was known as the *"navarra."* His wild and reckless style led to his fatal goring in 1801, a moment Goya also depicted in an etching — ***The Unlucky Death of Pepe Illo in the Madrid Bullring*** (*La desgraciada muerte de Pepe Illo en la plaza de Madrid).* He also painted seventeen pictures, six vignettes and two miniatures on diverse bullfighting themes, encapsulating specific moments of action in the ring and the atmosphere surrounding bullfights.

Between 1815 and 1816 he produced the series *La Tauromaquia* and in 1825, approaching the age of 80 and exiled in Bordeaux, drew the etchings that make up the series *Bulls of Bordeaux*. Together, they provide a record of the bullfighting of his day with precise detail of bullrings, the aficionados (fans), the *majas* (Spanish belles) watching from their balconies, the movements of the bullfighters, the fierceness of the bulls, the performance of the picadors and the many other aspects involved in the spectacle. His magnificent display of figures in movement can be likened to a series of photographs or even a film documentary.

In total, *La Tauromaquia* comprises forty etchings and aquatints, the plates for which are kept in the National Museum of Chalcography. The first thirteen are devoted to the history of bullfighting, from the Moors supporting the fighters in the ring to the participation of knights and nobility. Nicolás Fernández de Moratín describes El Cid's supposed application for a licence to take part in the show as follows:

> On a bay horse, covered in gold and finery,
> he requested an
> urban licence,
> to spear a bull.[24]

This legendary bullfight is reproduced in Goya's print of the *Cid Campeador Spearing Another Bull (El Cid Campeador lanceando a otro toro)*.

---

[24] Sobre un caballo alazano,
cubierto de galas y oro,
demanda licencia urbano,

The following prints reflect occasions when Goya was actually present at bullfights in Zaragoza:

The very skilful student of Falces, wrapped in his cape, tricks the bull with the play of his body (*El diestrísimo estudiante de Falces, embozado, burla al toro con sus quiebros*).

This bullfighter, who used the name of his native Navarran village, is dressed in the attire of his day and shows his skill at reducing the bull without even removing his cape.   A friend of Goya's, Martincho fought recklessly, almost like a circus act, as the painter depicted in three separate etchings:

- ***The famous Martincho places the banderillas playing the bull with the movement of his body*** (*El famoso Martincho poniendo banderillas al quiebro*).
- ***The daring of Martincho in the ring at Zaragoza*** [*Temeridad de Martincho en la plaza de Zaragoza*] where the matador receives the bull as it leaves the bull pens, seated with his feet shackled and ready to pierce the animal with his sword in a brutal clash.
- ***Another madness of his in the same ring*** (*Otra locura suya en la misma plaza*) where he is sitting on a table, also with his feet shackled and ready to pounce on the bull as it gores the table.

Another etching ***Manly courage of the celebrated 'Pajuelera' in the ring at Zaragoza*** (*Valor varonil de la célebre Pajuelera en la plaza de Zaragoza*), featuring the female picador mentioned above fiercely lancing the bull in the back of the neck.

The masquerade performance (*La función de la mojiganga*) presents a scene intended to make the audience laugh with a coach drawn by two donkeys with two buffoons on their backs lancing

para lancear un toro.

the bull as it gores one of the donkeys. Another buffoon puts his hand out of the window to stab the bull with *banderillas* while another two in the back of the carriage wave the *banderillas* they are about to plunge into the animal.

In one of his letters to Martín Zapater, who he knew was unwell in 1784, Goya says: "You have much business to attend to and you physically need to come to Madrid; you could leave it all behind and come and see a few bullfights and comedies here and you would have a very good laugh at everything."

In the eighteenth century, as in other periods in history, bullfighting was a subject of considerable controversy. It had opponents like Gaspar de Jovellanos, José Moñino, Benito Jerónimo Feijoo and José Cadalso, and advocates like Nicolás Fernandez de Moratín.

In 1785, the Count of Aranda, with royal blessing, introduced a ban on bullfighting except where it was considered to be in the public interest or for charitable purposes. That ban was lifted by Charles IV in 1793. Given his passion for bullfighting, Goya was a prominent participant in the protests against its prohibition. He argued that these spectacles were a major source of income for the Casa de la Misericordia charity, and contributed funding to care for orphans, the mentally ill and other people in need.

In another anecdote about his enthusiasm for the sport, Vicente López was painting a portrait of Goya commissioned by Ferdinand VII on his final visit to Madrid at the age of 80. Tired and growing impatient with the long sessions, Goya promised to show López a few artistic moves with the bullfighter's cape which he remembered from his youth, if he would only just hurry up and finish.

Goya's servant also left a record of the artist's passion for bullfighting: "My master was incorrigible on two counts: his fondness for bullfighting and his fondness for the daughters of Eve." Taking all of this into account, it is somewhat surprising that curators of the "Goya, Drawings" exhibition at the Prado Museum from December 2019 to February 2020, should have arrived at the conclusion that Goya was against bullfighting. In this magnificent show, the prints were admirably arranged in 23 rooms with perfect lighting and colour on the walls, and intelligent positioning of the prints, yet the curators made no reference to the hundreds of comments and texts written by distinguished art critics and scholars of Goya and his age. And yet, for whatever reason, they appeared to overstep their role by making the unsupported claim that Goya was against bullfighting.

Indeed, many scholars have disagreed with any such interpretation. A case in point is art history professor and Goya expert, Arturo Ansón Navarro, who explains:

> There is no contradiction between the clearly dramatic reproduction of bullfighting scenes and the appreciation of the animal in itself, and this does not mean [Goya] is insensitive to the animal's suffering. But to suggest this is an anti-bullfighting depiction is quite absurd and is to take it out of context and view it from what we might call a modern perspective.

For his part, historian Álvaro Martínez Novillo asserts:

> Throughout his life, Goya put a good deal of time and effort into depicting the 'Fiesta' [bullfighting] and such dedication would be neither coherent nor logical in a person who opposed

bullfighting. He reflects what he has seen without shying away from the violence or the horror.

At the exhibition of *La Tauromaquia* in the San Fernando Academy of Fine Arts in 2016, Juan Bordés, Academy Delegate at the National Chalcography Museum stated that it could not reasonably be claimed that any of the prints in this series would justify Goya's radical opposition to the bullfighting tradition and adds: "One need only see the beauty with which he draws the animal and the darkness of its surroundings to grasp what he was thinking."

Throughout his life, Goya dedicated a great deal of time to pictures, drawings, tapestries, lithography, and vignettes at a time when bullfighting had no academic relevance. This can only be explained by his passion for the sport.

Bullfighting may not appeal to all, but is a passion that can perhaps be equated to a love of mathematics, as defined by mathematician Mariano Mataix: "Not only are [maths] fun, they can even become a drug. But a salutary and beneficial drug, unlike those we are used to hearing about in daily life." Another mathematician Julio Rey Pastor claimed that where such an understanding of the subject was concerned, "a case of ineptitude [...] cannot be overcome with piles of printed paper. It is more prudent to recommend giving up." Perhaps those who are not equipped to study or understand bullfighting would also be better advised to turn their attention to other subjects.

The Theatre

In antiquity, Greek and Roman plays and tragedies were represented in ancient amphitheatres in Spain. But Zaragoza was one of the first cities to put on theatrical productions of Spanish creation. In 1414, when Ferdinand I was crowned King of Aragón in the Seo Cathedral, the plays staged were in the common language of his day. Over the years, theatre often led to brawls, riots, and even popular uprisings, leading the authorities to restrict content to religious themes performed inside the cathedral to mark special feast days on the ecclesiastical calendar, like Christmas.

In Zaragoza, plays were first performed in a *corral de comedias* or theatrical courtyard which the Council rented from the impresario. So, in 1589, the directors of the Hospital of Nuestra Señora de Gracia requested authorization to build the Casa de Comedias, a playhouse that was to be built on a plot of land in Calle del Coso. The profits were to go to the hospital's charitable work, and permission was granted.

Towards the middle of the sixteenth century, the playwright and author Lope de Rueda — considered the founder of Spanish theatre as a proponent of New Comedy — was writing works on religious themes and the nobility, although it was his *pasos* or interludes, farces and comedies that brought him fame and fortune. He used the local vernacular and depicted typical characters and customs of his day in comic episodes which played to large audiences and was the precursor of the great classical authors of the Spanish Golden Age like Lope de Vega, Calderón de la Barca, Tirso de Molina and many others who turned to themes of love, nobility, duels, family quarrels and other subjects relevant to the people of their day.

In the eighteenth century, when Goya was a young man in Zaragoza, theatrical performances were still based on classical themes and passion plays, particularly those of Calderón de la Barca. Into these plays were inserted *pasos* and *entremés* — like those written by Cervantes — where the leading characters are ordinary people, villains, prostitutes, and tricksters who used common casual language to discuss topical everyday subjects to the delight of their audiences.

The Calle del Coso playhouse was beside the Hospital lodge and Calle de la Soledad. Men and women accessed their separate seats in the courtyard and galleries through different doors. The women, accommodated in the circle colloquially known as "the pot", covered their faces with masks. The musketeers followed the play on foot and the halberdiers directed the audience, leading the applause or whistling directed at the playwright or actors, accompanied by bells, keys and other noisy instruments. Sometimes mice or lizards would be let loose in the 'pot' causing havoc among the female spectators.

A decline in audiences led to the introduction of more frivolous genres like one-act farces and *entremés*, and the inclusion of performances by beautiful young actresses who danced and sang *tonadillas* to great acclaim. As we shall see below, Goya himself witnessed one of the big theatrical scandals of his day involving actors, spectators, promotors, and some of the senior authorities at the time.

The excellent and beautiful actress María Ladvenant was performing Calderón de la Barca's comedy *"Afectos de odio y amor"* with her company in Zaragoza, to bring the season to a close. At the end of the show, the audience was enraptured and cried out for an encore, but the actress had already left the theatre and the mayor signalled the performance was over. The audience, however, refused to leave and such was the uproar that followed that the Captain General of Aragón and Regent of the Real Audiencia, who was among the spectators, decided to send his coach to the hotel to bring back the actress, who performed the reprise for her ecstatic fans.

This led to a major conflict of jurisdiction between the Captain General and the mayor appointed by the King. To settle the dispute, the President of the Spanish Military Tribunal, the Count of Aranda, intervened on the mayor's behalf, ordering the actress be imprisoned for four days. But Ladvenant had already left for the royal court. The following year, the managers of the Royal Hospital of Nuestra Señora de Gracia called on the Count of Aranda to authorize a repeat performance by the actress, but to no avail. Another factor may also have been the gossip at the time about the actress's relationship with the son of the Count of Fuentes, José María Pignatelli, who was married to the Count of Aranda's daughter.

Another popular actress in Goya's day was María Antonia Fernández, nicknamed La Caramba, and rival of La Tirana, a famed actress whose name is a popular song, but also means tyrant. La Caramba was an excellent actress and singer who also danced most gracefully, and Goya painted several portraits of her. Her youth, beauty, saucy songs, and voluptuous dancing delighted the crowds who flocked to see her. Promiscuous in her private life, her songs were condemned by many, including the young Duchesses of Alba and Osuna, who considered them a public scandal.

As a result, La Caramba chose to tour towns further away from Madrid and, on the advice of Goya, who is said to have been a close friend, she began her tour in Zaragoza, a city renowned for its love of the theatre and its big audiences. Her best-known song, and the one to which she owed her stage name, recounted how a foppish young gentleman sought to win her heart with tender compliments:

> "María Antonia, don't be such a tyrant
> Look my dear, how I love and adore you
> You shall have buckets of money"
> So, I answered him with my song
> Appealing to him with my singing and dancing:
> "How stubborn you are, fine gentleman!
> What you want is...?
> *Caramba! Caramba!*"
> [Oh goodness me, my goodness me!][25]

The impresario at the Zaragoza playhouse sought permission from the Captain General for La Caramba to perform in the intervals between plays. Permission was granted, but the mayor restricted her presence to performances over a very limited number of days. The hospital governor presented a letter to the municipal council, asking to increase the period allowed in view of the revenue it would bring for the hospital's charitable work, particularly as King Philip V had passed a recommendation by Royal Charter to ensure the playhouse's earnings be donated to the hospital. The authorization was finally given and La Caramba was allowed to perform all season, boosting the hospital's funds quite considerably.

That was the last occasion La Caramba performed. On her return to Madrid, she took shelter from a storm in the Capuchin church on Carrera de San Jerónimo one Sunday. A friar was

---

[25]   María Antonia, no seas tan tirana, Mira niña que te amo y te adoro
  Y tendrás las pesetas a manta, Yo le respondí con mi sonete,
  Con mi canto, mi baile y soflama: ¡Qué porfiado es V. señorito!
  ¿Usted quiere...? ¡Caramba, Caramba!

preaching a sermon on the frivolity of earthly goods and chattels when compared to the delight of spiritual life, and La Caramba promptly decided to withdraw from public life. From that point, she led a life of penitence until her premature death.

In 1778, a raging fire consumed the playhouse — which had capacity for 1,300 people — during a performance of the opera "Artaxerxes." There were two hundred casualties, both dead and wounded. The adjacent mental asylum which Goya painted in **Fire at Night** (*El incendio de noche)* and **The Madhouse** (*Casa de locos)* also caught fire. In 1791, a year before he went deaf, and on sick leave granted by Charles IV, Goya attended the inauguration of the new replacement theatre where "The Tetrarch of Jerusalem" was being performed.

A lover of both theatre and music, Goya cultivated friendships with authors, actors, and musicians of his day. In his Costumbrist farces featuring everyday life, Goya's friend and contemporary, the dramatist Ramón de la Cruz depicts, in the style of Cervantes *entremés*, the facets, virtues and failings of Spanish people in the eighteenth century, just as Goya did in his drawings. Both men bore witness to the social context that defined the authentic Spain of their day.

Later, in 1799 and 1824, Goya painted his friend Leandro Fernández de Moratín, with whom he formed a friendship that would last into his final days in Bordeaux, where the two men coincided in exile. Goya also made drew on Moratín's works and comments as a source of inspiration in his drawings, particularly for **La Tauromaquia** series and the captions accompanying them.

Goya's friendships and relationships with prominent theatrical figures in Zaragoza and later Madrid, also gave rise to the following works.

- Two portraits in 1799 and 1824 of **Leandro Fernández de Moratín**, dramatist, poet, and friend.

- Two portraits of **María Rosario Fernández "La Tirana"**, considered the leading performer of her day and the favourite of many enlightened authors. The first, from 1794, is a half-length portrait, where she is depicted with a white complexion, white floral dress, and thick black hair with a red rose. The second, from 1799, is a full-length portrait, where she is wearing a light white dress with an open neckline and is covered in a red mantle.

- Three portraits of **Isidro Máiquez**, born in 1768 and considered the best actor of the eighteenth century. He performed with the great actresses of his day, like La Tirana and Rita Luna. He renovated the theatre of the time and gave magnificent performances of Shakespeare's "Othello", Calderón de la Barca's "Life is a Dream" and Cervantes' "Numancia", to name part of his vast repertoire. He was also a writer and theatre director. He suffered reprisals for his enlightened attitude after the Peninsular War, was imprisoned in 1814 and banished from the Court.

- A portrait of his close friend Rita Luna, the whereabouts of which is unknown: the actress is sitting in a meadow of flowers with a barking poodle in front of her; at the bottom of the picture, Goya wrote a caption which read: "dogs bark at the Luna (Moon) because they cannot bite her." He painted a voluptuous **Rita Luna** on another occasion as Judith in **Judith and Holofernes**, one of the Black Paintings that graced the walls of his *Quinta del Sordo* villa.

- Several portraits of actors entitled **Portrait of an Unknown Gentleman** *(Caballero desconocido)*.

- A portrait of **Lorenza Correa**, a leading soprano who toured Europe's main opera houses, including Paris, where she performed for Napoleon, Rome, and La Scala in Milan where Rossini dedicated his opera "Aureliano in Palmira" to her.

- A portrait of the beautiful **Rita Molinos**, actress and singer condemned for her alleged relationship with Godoy. It is a sensual, half-length portrait where she is dressed in a black lace dress and mantilla shawl. Her head is leaning on her right arm and her look is one of fatigue.
- **The Strolling Players** (*Cómicos ambulantes*), dedicated to one of the theatre companies which toured village fairs. This picture was painted on tin plate in 1793, on Goya's return from the serious illness from which he spent time recuperating in Murcia. He claimed he had painted it "to occupy my mortified imagination by considering my ills and to partially compensate for the great disbursements they have caused me."
- A portrait of his friend, the Enlightenment writer and poet **Juan Meléndez Valdés** who, like Goya, died in exile in France.

Tertulias

Rather like salons, *tertulias* were social gatherings in the homes of the urban upper and middle classes. At these informal meetings, participants discussed current affairs, engaged in flirtation, games of forfeits, poetry recitals and the reading of sayings and proverbs, all washed down with a great deal of food and drink. Performers would sometimes be invited to sing arias or play musical instruments, particularly the violin. In Zaragoza, Goya was introduced into the salon world by the Bayeu brothers and his friend Martín Zapater, and it was here that he would meet Martín de Goicoechea.

In Madrid, he frequented the tertulias in the Fonda de San Sebastián tavern, where conversation was restricted to "theatre, bullfighting, love and verse." Goya took great delight in the eloquent contributions made by Jovellanos. Particularly famous were the salons organized by the Countess-Duchess of Benavente who was attracted by the conversation enlivened by José Cadalso, considered Spain's first Romantic author.

Later, the *tertulias* would move on to subjects related to revolutionary and cultural events in France, and entry became more restricted. In Goya's house, a group of Enlightenment advocates would often gather, and captions for Goya's prints were often suggested and discussed.

In 1793, Goya overcame the serious illness which struck him, but was left stone deaf as a result, and was no longer able to take part in these social occasions.

Romerías and Picnics in the Country

Popular with ordinary folk, these were either religious in nature, which involved walking to a chapel near Zaragoza, or secular to celebrate special occasions like the completion of the Imperial Canal.

Meriendas or picnics were joyful days of courtship and flirtation among young people, with games and dancing, food, and drink. One such occasion is depicted by Goya in the magnificent **Meadow of San Isidro in Madrid** (*La pradera de San Isidro de Madrid*).

Taking a Stroll

Afternoon strolls in the woodland around the Monastery of Santa Engracia were popular with Zaragozans, and on feast days like Saint John's, the military bands of the regiments quartered in the city would provide musical accompaniment. When the weather was fine, people would walk along the paths on the banks of the river Ebro.

On feast days in the city, nocturnal serenatas would be sung up to the balconies of young women in their homes, and coplas would be accompanied by clarinets, small drums, flutes, and guitars. These musical sessions sometimes ended in trouble, with fights breaking out between the young men.

Shows and Exhibitions

Painting and sculpture by well-known artists would often go on show in the city. There were also performances by small travelling companies with musical and circus acts designed to amaze the spectator, like the prowess of the strongman, the exhibition of conjoined twins from Igualada with three shared legs, or the French balloonists who kept their huge balloon up in the air for seven minutes. The amateur status of some of the troupes would often lead to cancellation with the subsequent protests and commotion this provoked.

In addition to the authorized shows, improvised venues sometimes sprang up, like a fake chapel in Torrero, beside Gypsy Cave, where all kinds of disreputable nocturnal activities and excesses led to its closure.

Music

Goya was a great music enthusiast. He attended opera in the Teatro de la Comedia, and concerts and aria recitals in the Seo Cathedral and the Basilica of El Pilar. When his friend Zapater came to see him in Madrid, he often invited him out to the opera. He was friends with counter tenor Pedro Mocarte, the composer Manuel Quijano and divas like the aforementioned La Tirana and Rita Luna. He also became acquainted with the compositions of Bocherini, whom he met at the palace of Don Luis of Arenas de San Pedro and painted in a picture dedicated to the family of María Teresa de Vallabriga, into which Goya also painted himself.

On turbulent evenings and nights of wine and revelry in Zaragoza's taverns, especially after a bullfight, Goya would accompany the popular songs and dances of tiranas and boleras with the guitar. On many of these merry evenings, he would spend time with singer Pedro Mocarte, whom he called "Periquillo" and had known since a boy in Zaragoza. Pedro was in the children's choir school at the Basilica of El Pilar. When his voice changed, he became a counter tenor on a par with castrati like Farinelli and was a professional opera singer at Toledo Cathedral.

A fan of *jota de picadillo*, Goya would sometimes accompany songs on his guitar. He depicts *jota* dancing in his works **Masked Dance** (*Baile de máscaras)*, **Couple Dancing** (*Pareja bailando*) and **Watch that Step** (*Cuidado con ese paso*).

By 1790, when he was 44, Goya confessed to his friend Zapater that his age and social position now prevented him from taking part in this type of merriment. "The *seguidillas* I am happy to include, so that you can listen to them, but I cannot listen to them myself and will not do so, because, as you will imagine, I no longer go to the places I could hear them in order to preserve my dignity.

The Advent of War

Goya's life was undoubtedly affected by war, but he was no warmonger, and it was not a subject with which he engaged unless he was close to the horror of its consequences. His Aragonese and Spanish patriotism persuaded him to paint the tragedy of the Sieges of Zaragoza in his print series ***The Disasters of War***, when called upon by Palafox to provide a record of what had happened with the invasion of Napoleon's troops. The same patriotism gave rise to his epic painting of the uprising of ***The Second of May 1808*** and the executions of ***The Third of May 1808***. Manuel Machado wrote a poem about this second painting, of which this is an extract:

He saw them. Black night, hell's light
The stench of blood and gunpowder, groaning
Open arms, spreading
In this gesture of eternal pain,
A lamp on the ground almost illuminates
With a terrifying yellow halo,
the guns in the row of uniforms,
brutal and monotonous, in the half-light[26]

He did not paint the terrible yet decisive Battle of Trafalgar on 21 October 1805, when the Franco-Spanish navy was defeated

---

[26] Él los vio. Noche negra, luz de infierno
Hedor de sangre y pólvora, gemidos
Unos brazos abiertos, extendidos

by the English. Nor did he paint the war in Africa between 1774 and 1775, when the army of Moroccan Sultan Mohammed III, lay siege to the city of Melilla with British support, and was pushed back by the Spanish army of Charles III, backed by French troops. This led to the signing of the treaty of Aranjuez of 1780.

He also steered clear of painting Napoleon. The French emperor had invaded Spain, forced the abdication of the Spanish monarchs and was responsible for the terrible Peninsular War all of which, as a proud Spaniard, Goya condemned, despite his Enlightened and liberal ideas.

Nor did he depict the brave endeavours of the Spanish navy in their many battles against the Juntas de Indias — the local administrations in the Americas — which, having engaged with the formation of the Cortes of Cádiz legislative body, began a process of independence culminating in1828.

Neither did he paint the Spanish general and liberal politician Rafael del Riego nor depict the Hundred Thousand Sons of Saint Louis, a French army mobilized by Louis XVIII to support the absolute monarch, Ferdinand VII.

Politics

The decline in the power of the Spanish empire began in the sixteenth century. In the seventeenth century, Portugal separated from Spain and the Netherlands also declared independence.

En ese gesto de dolor eterno,
Una farola en tierra casi alumbra
Con un halo amarillo que horripila,
De los fusiles la uniforme fila,
monótona y brutal en la penumbra

The death of the last Habsburg king, Charles II, led to the War of the Spanish Succession with conflict between the Bourbons and the Carlists, leading to the eventual victory of the Bourbon Philip V, but at the expense of Spain's global significance, which dwindled on both the European and world stage. The Treaty of Utrecht of 1715 marked the end of the war, with Gibraltar handed over to the British and the end of Spanish control of the Mediterranean.

After the *Pactes de Famille* or Family Compacts, the first of which was agreed in El Escorial in 1733 by Philip V and Louis XV, an expedition was sent to Italy to put Charles, the son of Philip V and Elisabeth Farnese, on the throne of Naples. The Count of Montemar, whose mausoleum is in the Basilica of El Pilar, oversaw the army that took Naples and conquered Sicily, allowing Charles to be crowned in Palermo as King of the Two Sicilies, as we saw in Chapter 5.

Where domestic policy was concerned, Philip V strengthened the Bourbon aristocracy and the clergy, who were centralists, unlike the bourgeoisie and lower nobility who supported regional jurisdictions, like the *fuero* of Aragón. On the cultural level, Philip patronized the arts, as did his successors.

Charles III sent Giovani Battista Tiépolo to Spain, where the Baroque artist decorated the ceiling of the throne room in the Royal Palace of Madrid on the theme of Spain and its provinces. In 1761, he sent a ship to Italy to bring back the German neo-classical artist Mengs, who was resident in Rome, to make him first court painter. Mengs painted many pictures for the Royal Palaces of Madrid and Aranjuez.

When Charles III reached Spain from Naples, new liberal and Enlightenment ideas were spreading across Europe, backed by many politicians, clergy, and members of the nobility. Goya also engaged with these ideas, but painting was his life and he continued to cultivate friendships with — and paint portraits of — both conservatives like Floridablanca and Enlightenment advocates like Jovellanos.

From Philip V to Charles IV, the Bourbon monarchs continued to renew titles, consolidating the nobility, and shoring up their own power, but the implementation of the right of primogeniture led to many *hidalgos* losing their privileged economic situation. Unlike in France, the Enlightened clergy remained loyal to the king, with exceptions like Cardinal Luis María of Bourbon y Vallabriga, who took part in the Cortes of Cádiz assembly and supported the Liberal Triennium of Rafael de Riego, the three-year period when the liberal government was in power after an uprising against the absolutist Ferdinand VII.

Goya also supported the new ideas of freedom and popular democracy which Napoleon stood for, but when he witnessed the brutal and vandalistic behaviour of his troops and realised that the French emperor had intended to subjugate the Spanish people, his patriotism was reawakened, and he recorded the horrors of war in his pictures. However, he was not active in political organizations, nor did he hold any political post. More than a revolutionary, he was a reformist and believed that political solutions must be gradual, rather than breaking violently with the past.

His strong character and short temper often affected his sound judgement and his few declarations on politics and religion. Keeping a deliberate distance was a priority in his life and work and enabled him to depict subjects that ranged from the popular working classes to the aristocracy, the religious, the revolutionary, and the pacifist. The importance to him of his work as an artist and his non-affiliation to political or religious doctrines allowed him to be even-handed in his treatment of feelings and behaviour. His religious paintings reflect his devotion to the Virgin of the Pillar and his respect for the figures of Christianity, but he was equally capable of the realistic depiction of death, with people reduced to nothing, and to mercilessly criticize immoral or ignorant religious figures. Goya's desire for self-development and happiness, and to reach his full potential socially and economically, ultimately prevailed over his political and religious ideas and private pleasures.

That distance, in addition to his good relations with the powers-that-be enabled him to paint, not only monarchs and royalty, but also the representative in Spain of the French Revolution, Joseph Bonaparte, who was briefly King of Spain. So too he painted politicians of different ideologies, Prime Minister Godoy, the fearless Spanish guerrilla and general known as *El Empecinado*, sent to the gallows by Ferdinand VII, and military men from different armed forces who fought in Spain, like Palafox, and Napoleon's General Guye.

This varied scenario gave him the chance to produce great works, but also caused him moments of difficulty, such as when he accepted the Royal Order of Spain. Contemptuously known as the "Order of the Aubergine" for its purple colour, it was awarded to Goya by Joseph I for portraying him on the medallion in the picture ***Allegory of the City of Madrid*** (*Alegoría de la Villa de Madrid*). However, the painter from Aragón never wore the medal, as the portrait had been painted by one of his assistants. When Joseph I, contemptuously referred to as "Pepe Botella" by his opponents, lost the war and fled from Spain, Goya had it overpainted. The oval was subsequently painted and repainted on several occasions, in line with historical events, and eventually covered with the legend "Second of May."

Goya's acquaintance and friendship with the family of Charles IV saved his life when Charles's son Ferdinand VII threatened to send him to the gallows for his liberal ideas, but ultimately forgave him so that he could continue with his portrait. Goya lived more in fear of the Inquisition than the King and, faced with its constant persecution, he sought refuge in the house of his friend the Aragonese canon José Duaso y Latre, director of the Royal Hospital of Buen Suceso in Madrid and the King's chaplain of honour, of whom he also painted a severe but honest portrait.

In May 1823, the Duke of Angoulême had recaptured Madrid on behalf of Ferdinand VII, and it was on this date that his absolute monarchy was restored. In the resulting repression, Goya requested royal permission to depart for the French spa of Plombiers for health reasons, and his plea was granted. In fact, he moved to Bordeaux in 1824 and only returned briefly to Madrid in 1827 to settle his pension of fifty thousand *reales*.

Languages

Goya put all his time and effort into perfecting his technique and work. But when another activity attracted his interest he engaged with it intellectually, learning and practising his new skill. He drew on his knowledge of Latin, for instance, to produce the captions that accompany his prints.

In private classes, he acquired considerable mastery of French, which he spoke and wrote fluently, as his friend the polyglot Bernardo de Iriarte attested in a letter to Zapater, and as he demonstrated in the final years of his life in Bordeaux and his trip to Paris.

He practised Italian during his trip of several months to Rome and other parts of Italy and used it in a letter he wrote to the Count of Carlo Dalla Torre, accompanying his entry for the Parma competition stating the theme he had chosen on 20 April 1771.

Reading

Goya certainly read Cervantes and depicted a various scene from *Don Quixote* in his work. One example is his drawing of two shepherdesses exclaiming "I think." This is a reference to the "I am free" speech given by Marcela in the pastoral episode who, when pursued by a suitor, asserts her own free will to resolve the conflict posed by feelings of love. In this passage, Cervantes describes the burial of the rich young *hidalgo* Crysostom turned shepherd, who has died for the unrequited love of the beautiful but elusive Marcela. She, though rich, has opted to live among shepherdesses so she can be part of their candid conversations as they take care of their goats. At the burial, Marcela speaks out thus: "I was born free, and to live free I chose the solitude of the fields." She refuses to take responsibility for Crysostom's death, saying: "I do not understand why, merely because she has inspired love, a woman who is loved for her beauty is obliged to love the man who loves her."

Goya also produced a copper plate, found recently, which illustrates the "Braying adventure", in the 1780 Ibarra edition of *Don Quixote* which the Royal Spanish Academy chose not to include in its version.

Goya was a great reader and took inspiration for his work from many books. His library contained hundreds of volumes, and he also had access to other libraries like those of the Count and Countess of Fuentes in Zaragoza and Madrid, those of the Duke and Duchess of Alba and Osuna, and the Royal Library.

For his **Black Paintings**, he drew on the work of **Fernández Moratín**, writer, poet and *acalófilo* (a Madrid salon with a focus on ugliness). In one account, later depicted by Goya, this writer relates the trial in Logroño in 1610 of the members of a witches' sect which used to meet in their coven in "Buck's Meadow." They were condemned by the Inquisition to be burned at the stake for their purification.

As we have seen, Goya regularly attended the Zaragoza Playhouse, where all kinds of musical and theatrical shows took place, including plays by his good friend Ramón de la Cruz.

When his wife Josefa Bayeu died in1812, he had the family library valued for 1500 *reales*, a figure that suggests it contained hundreds of books, from many of which he drew the inspiration for the content and captions of his paintings and prints.

In Goya's lifetime, freedom to print was limited for many years by the Inquisition. Press freedom did exist briefly between 1810 and 1814, but Ferdinand VI abolished it again by decree and reinstated the Inquisition. The final stage of his absolutist monarchy, between 1823 and 1833, was particularly appalling in this regard.

The following are some of the subjects dealt with by the books in Goya's library and which we see reflected in his works

- Animals

  "El Asno Erudito" (The Erudite Ass) is a book by Juan Pablo Forner, of 1782, and appears in Goya's print **And so was his grandfather** *(Asta su abuelo).*

  "La Carta Apologética" (The Apologetic Letter) by José de Gomarusa dealt with bullfighting.

"Carta histórica sobre el origen y progresos de las fiestas de toros en España" (Historical Letter on the Origin and Progress of Bullfighting in Spain) by Nicolás Fernández de Moratín of 1777.

One of the "Fables" of Félix María de Samaniego is depicted in Goya's etching **Strange Devotion** (*Extraña devoción)* where a donkey is laden with relics.

"Glianimaliparlanti" by Giovanni Battista Casti of 1801, contains a poem used for the libretto of the eponymous opera. The figure of the wolf is used in the etching **This is the worst of it** *(Esto es lo peor)* from the **Disasters of War** series.

- Witches

  "Auto de fe celebrado en la ciudad de Logroño los días seis y siete de noviembre de 1610" by Leandro Fernández de Moratín, featuring the witch trial episode related above, appears with similar texts in some Goya etchings.

- The clergy

  According to the 1787 census, in Goya's day there were 142,283 clergymen, of which half were regular clergy living in 2,067 monasteries, while the remainder were secular clergy or ordained ministers who did not belong to a religious order. Goya portrayed their extravagance and vices in many of his prints.

  "Cartas marruecas" (Moroccan Letters) by Cadalso.

  "Conversaciones instructivas entre el padre fray Bertoldo capuchino y D. Terencio" by Fray Francisco de los Arcos, a book banned by the Spanish Inquisition.

  "Fray Gerundio de Campazas" by the Jesuit José Francisco de Isla, also banned by the Inquisition, and used by Goya in his prints **What a golden beak!** *(¡Que pico de* *oro!*) and ***Might not the pupil know more?*** [¿Sabrá más el discípulo?]

"Dómine Lucas" by José de Cañizares was used in the *Capricho* print ***The Chinchillas*** *(Los chinchillas).*

Samaniego's poem "Description of the Carmelite Convent of Bilbao called features in ***They Are Hot*** (*Están Calientes*) which depicts the excessive amounts of food and wine consumed at the monastery.

"Los desahuciados del mundo y la gloria" by Tomás Villaroel.

- Customs and traditions

"La Serafina", novel by José Mor de Fuentes, born in Monzón (Huesca) in 1762 deals with popular Madrid customs.

"Nova Iconologia" by Cesare Ripa is the source for Goya's allegorical pictures ***Poetry*** (*La poesía*) and ***Truth, Time, and History*** *(La Verdad, el Tiempo y la Historia).*

Cervantes's picaresque novels

"Óptica del cortejo" by Ramírez de Góngora which includes critical and moralizing fragments on the debauchery of that time. Goya drew on it to condemn contemporary follies and foolishness.

"Sainetes" by Ramón de la Cruz may well have inspired some of his tapestry cartoons.

"Sátira a Amesto" by Jovellanos, on marriages of convenience, which feature in his picture ***The Wedding*** *(La boda).*

- Goblins

"Conversaciones instructivas sobre duendes y disparates" by Fray Francisco de los Arcos.

"Duendes y espíritus familiares" and "Sobre la multitude de los milagros" by Benito Jerónimo Feijoo, a pre-Enlightenment Benedictine monk who was decorated by Ferdinand VI and Charles III in recognition of his love for his homeland. He was considered the Spanish Voltaire, although violence did not feature in his work. Menéndez Pelayo claimed Feijoo had freed himself from the rigidities of scholasticism and preconceived systems. Goya shared this notion and stated in his report to the San Fernando Royal Academy of Fine Arts in 1792 that "lack of talent is the only criterion that might permit us to argue in favour of norms, systems and rules."

"Pan y toros" (Bread and Bulls), by León del Arroyal, a secretly distributed reformist tract which claimed that the true *duendes* (or goblins) in this world were the priests and friars who ate and drank at the people's expense. It was used for the Capricho **No one has seen us** (*Nadie nos ha visto*).

- The Inquisition

  The subject of many books and articles kept in Goya's library, it was also a theme in many of his etchings. One is his drawing of Voltaire with its caption "Meurs impie ou pense comme moi."

- Nobility

  "Memorias de la insigne Academia Asnal" by Doctor Ballesteros. The etching on this book "Asinus Nobilis" was the basis for his Capricho **As far back as his grandfather** (*Hasta su abuelo*).

  "Lugubrious Nights" and "Moroccan Letters" by José Cadalso were the origin of the etching in defence of the Constitution of Cádiz entitled **Lux ex tenebris.**

  "Sobre la nobleza, señorios y los mayorazgos" (On Nobility, Estates and Entailments) by the Count of Cabarrús.

"Valor de la nobleza e influjo de la sangre" (The Value of Nobility and the Influence of the Blood) by Benito Feijoó.

- Prostitution

  "El arte de las putas" (The Art of Whores), a poem by Nicolás Fernández de Moratín

  "La Celestina" or The Tragicomedy of Calisto and Melibea, attributed to Fernando de Rojas, served as inspiration for many of the drawings and captions in Los Caprichos, such as **She prays for her** (*Ruega por ella).*

  "Sátiras y diarios" (Satires and diaries) by Jovellanos, about religion and prostitutes. It is a subject that features in many etchings.

- Classical authors

  Goya drew on themes from mythology and classical authors which were the source of many of the sculptures and paintings he had studied in detail in Italy in 1771, and which he developed in the following works:

  Some mythological themes like **Sacrifice to Vesta** and **Sacrifice to Pan**,[27] (*Sacrificio a Vesta and Sacrificio a Pan),* are less carefully executed, unlike the impressive **Saturn Devouring His Son** (*Saturno devorando a uno de sus hijos),* painted on the walls of the villa Quinta del Sordo, where Goya powerfully expresses the horror and cruelty of the scene where Titan Cronus, beside himself, rips open the body of his son to devour him.

  In **The Feast of Esther and Ahasuerus** (*El festín de Ester y Asuero*) and **Aman's Pardon** (*El perdón de Amán*) Goya mixes the technique he had observed in Italian masters with his own approach to painting, with sketchi-

---

[27] Juan Antonio Gaya. Las pinturas mitológicas de Goya. Goya Revista de Arte No. 100. Madrid 1971.

er, faster brushstrokes. In Aman's Pardon, the almost theatrical gesture and expression of the figures is remarkable. The young Goya was already using the wide range of colours and shades he would perfect in later works.

One of his Black Paintings, ***Judith de Betulia*** evokes the story of the beautiful Jewish widow with whom the Assyrian king Holofernes — who has laid siege to the Jewish city of Bethulia — falls in love. She beheads him and brings about the victory of the Jewish army.

Atropos or The Fates (Átropos o Las Parcas) is based on the three Moirai, the goddesses who decided human destiny with the thread they carried in their hands. The colours and technique used in the painting are precursors of Expressionism.

Asmodea is based on a mythological theme, in shades of ochre, grey and black, and evokes the Persian demon of wrath Asmodeus, whose legend is recounted in the Hebrew Book of Tobit.

On Goya's experiences described in this chapter, many of which also feature in his letters to Zapater, Ángel Canellas states in "Diplomatario de Goya" that the painter from Aragón "maintained the difficult political position of a man torn between the popular cause and that of a select group of Francophiles", and that in "the highly original captions of his print collections, we find a Goya who is free from vulgarities and with a notable level of culture over which is drawn a veil because it is unknown."

Chapter 7

Goya's Work and Aragón

Throughout his life, Goya expressed undying love for his homeland of Aragón, which was always in his mind. He drew on his memories and experiences there in much of his work. After moving away from the region, he returned on a number of occasions and always demonstrated just how very Aragonese he was.

Rural life was ingrained on his memory in during his childhood in Fuendetodos, and is commemorated in many of his works: the landscapes of his tapestry cartoons, his portraits of hunters, the faces and actions of children, his depiction of bullfighting and popular games, country paths off the beaten track, women with children on their way to collect water from a fountain, billy goats and rams amidst the flocks of sheep featured in witches' sabbaths and other themes.

The memory of Goya's years in Zaragoza are apparent in the pictures he painted as an apprentice at the drawing academy. Initially, Neoclassical and Baroque in style, they were later enriched with the knowledge acquired from studying and contemplating the work of the classical artists he was able to view more closely on his trip to Italy. This contributed to his large-scale frescoes in the church of the Aula Dei Charterhouse, and the delicate shades painted in 1772 on the vault of the small choir of the Basilica of El Pilar, in his ***Adoration of the Name of God*** (*La adoración del nombre de Dios),* which marked the beginning of his own personal style, with dynamic, sketchy brushstrokes.

Goya returned to Zaragoza on a number of occasions to complete commissions, paint the portraits of distinguished Zaragozans and, of course, to visit his beloved family and dear friends like Martín Zapater or Goicoechea. Goya wasted no opportunity to connect his life, art and thoughts with his native region. The portrait of the architect ***Ventura Rodríguez*** painted

174

in 1784 was commissioned by María Teresa de Vallabriga, the Zaragozan wife of the Infante Luis of Bourbon. Goya included a symbolic representation of the sitter's profession, whom he depicted in a drawing of the Chapel of Our Lady of the Pillar which the architect, whose second wife was the Rita Garro of Zaragoza, was working on at the time. One of the Basilica's columns features in the background.

In Fuendetodos, Goya's family house looks directly out onto the countryside: even today, we can see the well, farmland and, less than a kilometre away, gentle, pine-covered hills. When, after his success at the court in Madrid, where he rubbed shoulders with the highest levels of power and the aristocracy, Goya decided to leave his home near the city centre in Puerta del Sol to escape the Inquisition, he bought a house in the country with its own farmland on the banks of the river Manzanares. His nostalgia for his childhood in Fuendetodos undoubtedly contributed to this change in his way of life.

According to Baticle, "his visceral ties to Aragón left an indelible mark on the particular nature and inspiration of his work. When Spanish authors refer to him as the Aragonese genius, they are referring to the way in which he differs from artists born in other provinces."

First in Fuendetodos and later in Zaragoza, Goya always stayed in contact with nature, rural life and the Aragonese landscape. In more prosaic matters, but nevertheless indicative of his predilection for his native countryside, he once asked Martin Zapater to send two Aragonese mules from Zaragoza to Madrid as they were, in his view, the best in Spain. His friend was happy to fulfil his request.

Goya painted more than 400 portraits. Some were self-portraits, but most of his sitters were from the worlds of politics, the nobility, the clergy, the Spanish, French and British military, friends who engaged in bullfighting, music, or the theatre, or who people he knew from his daily life.

The following is a chronological list of Goya's paintings in Aragón. A recent exhibition dedicated to Corrado Giaquinto in Spain which opened at the Fundación Ibercaja Goya Museum in Zaragoza on 25 June 2021, also included three new works attributed to Goya, entitled ***Our Lady of the Pillar with Saint James and a Convert from Zaragoza*** (*Virgen del Pilar con Santiago y uno de los convertidos zaragozanos*), ***Saint Christopher*** (*San Cristóbal*), and the ***Adoration in the Name of God or The Glory*** (*La Gloria o la adoración del nombre de Dios*).

1758 -1760

His first portrait is considered by some to be ***The Boy with a Bindle*** (*El Chico del Capazo*), a small oil painting measuring 0.31 x 0.24 metres. It depicts a boy aged about nine wearing rags and is typical of the children from poor families who carried out odd jobs for wealthier farmers like the Lucientes, Goya's mother's family, in exchange for food. These boys, who did not go to school, were kept busy with lighter chores, given their young age, like this portrait of the boy with a bindle over his shoulder suggests. They would take the farm horses to water after a hard day's work in the fields and prepare their feed and bedding straw in the stable where they would spend the night. They also took food to farmhands in the fields near the village and helped in the kitchen preparing the saddlebags when the workers had to travel further afield. Working days might start as early as four in the morning and end at ten at night. The boys also helped with threshing wheat and barley, putting it into sacks and other kinds of manual labour needed on the farm.

This early picture already reveals what was to become a common feature in Goya's portraits: his ability to depict not only the boy's physical appearance, but his spirit and character. With his large head, the boy looks prematurely aged, while his sad lips and eyes reflect the harsh life he has to endure, always at the beck and call, not only of the 'master' or farm owner, but of his wife and servants, whom he would be required to help in the kitchen and with other domestic chores, and who may not have been kind about his features.

The Blond Girl (*La Niña Rubia*) is a small oil painting on tin measuring 0.32 x 0.24 metres. This extraordinary picture dates from Goya's early years as a painter, at the age of thirteen, shortly after arriving in Zaragoza, where he would have met his model, possibly a daughter of the Count and Countess of Fuentes.

The portrait depicts the graceful blond head of a small girl, whose upper torso is covered in white gauze. Parted in the centre, her hair falls dishevelled over her shoulders. Spots of yellow gleam in the background, outlining the girl's face and creating a sense of movement towards the viewer. Her round pupils and the bright white dot in her iris add character, as if she was scrutinizing the artist's technique as he worked, conjuring up a close, enigmatic connection between sitter and painter. Her wide-eyed gaze on the world and large, pretty eyes combine with a smile that evokes curiosity, kindness, and charm. Even as a teenager, Goya achieves a magic on a par with some of the great masters. He was to return to this gaze and physiognomy, with different nuances, in later portraits of children:

- **Mariano Goya**. R Portrait of his grandson as a boy, whom he endows with a sharply intelligent expression
- **The Family of Charles IV** *La familia de Carlos IV)* In this magnificent and well-known work, the monarchs' younger

son, the Infante Francisco de Paula Antonio, shares similar features, although his expression is more solemn and dignified, as perhaps befits his royal lineage.

- ***The Duke and Duchess of Osuna and their children*** *(Los duques de Osuna y sus hijos).* The little girl holding her mother's left hand would later become the Marchioness of Santa Cruz, whom Goya later portrayed. She wears a similar hairstyle, parted in the middle, to that early portrait of the blond girl; her gaze and smile have an aristocratic aspect which enhances the likeness.

- ***Victor Guye***, nephew of a French general in Napoleon's army, who was to be sent to the court of Joseph I, features the same childlike expression.

1762

The painting of the reliquary doors in Fuendetodos Church, discussed earlier marks the starting point for many of Goya's later paintings. The Baroque style and linear strokes resemble those of his master Luzán in other churches. The same light, figures and atmosphere were recovered twenty years later in the magnificent ***Apparition of the Virgin of the Pillar to Saint James and the Converted*** (*Aparición de la Virgen del Pilar a Santiago y los convertidos)* for the church of Urrea de Gaén, which was destroyed in the Spanish Civil War, but of which a photograph, sketch and preparatory drawing still exist. Giaquinto's influence is apparent here in the execution of the bearded men and the loose brushwork.

The same year, he painted ***Consecration of Aloysius Gonzaga as patron saint of youth*** (*La Consagración de San Luis Gonzaga como Patrono de la Juventud).*

1763

The painting ***The Triple Generation*** *(La Sagrada Familia y el Padre Eterno)* clearly draws on that early painting on the reliquary doors in Fuendetodos, although Goya has progressed to other techniques and forms. Here, the angel bearing the cloud is similar to the fresco painted by Antonio González Velázquez on the vault of the Basilica's Holy Chapel, in 1752.

1766 -1767

In early 1766, Goya painted ***Exaltation of the Name of Jesus*** *(Exaltación del nombre de Jesús)* on the stair vault in the old Jesuit school in Alagón, Zaragoza, a clear precursor of the fresco painted in 1772 in the small choir or *coreto* of the Basilica of El Pilar.

In his application for a scholarship to study in Italy, Goya presented a picture to the San Fernando Royal Academy of Fine Arts on the following theme: "Martha, Empress of Constantinople, in Burgos requesting a third of the sum set by the Sultan of Egypt for the ransom of her husband Emperor Baldwin from King Alfonso the Wise. The Spanish monarch ordered that she be given the whole sum." On 22 July, the jury added an extra theme to be completed in two hours, namely "Juan de Urbino and Diego de Paredes in discussion in Italy, on seeing the Spanish army, to decide which of them should have the weapons of the Marquis of Pescara." Neither of the works entered by Goya received a single vote in the competition, which was won by his future brother-in-law, Ramón Bayeu.

This was also the time when Goya decorated the pendentives of the vault over the transept of the Jesuit Church of San Juan

Bautista in Calatayud with the series entitled ***The Fathers of the Western Church***. The same theme, painted in the delicate shades of Italian Rococo style, would later feature in paintings in the Aragonese villages of Muel and Remolinos.

Also in the same year, Goya produced some small pictures on the ***Esquilache Riots*** *(Motín de Esquilache)*. The first reflects his approach to drawing groups, details, and legends. The uprisings were the result of food prices and anger against the foreign ministers brought in by Charles III. The Esquilache Riots had their Zaragozan equivalent in the Bread or *Broqueleros* Riot when homes and storehouses were ransacked and set on fire. When the authorities failed to act, the archbishop processed the Holy Sacrament through the central parishes of San Felipe and San Gilin a bid to restore the peace. However, the procession did not have the intended results, and although the rioters initially calmed down and knelt before the monstrance, no sooner had it moved on than they returned to their pillaging and destruction. On a similar theme, the lost oil painting ***Night procession of the Host through the streets of Zaragoza*** *(Procesión nocturna del Santísimo por las calles de Zaragoza)* is also attributed to Goya. Given the situation, a group of some fifty citizens decided to take matter into their own hands to restore order and, armed with ancient swords known as *broqueles* belonging to their ancestors, they confronted and forcibly pacified the crowd. The picture highlights the different protagonists that night. In the foreground is a man of virile and elegant appearance, perhaps one of the so-called *broqueleros* who would later turn to such violence, at the front of the procession beside the banner, holding a candle flag as a sign of faith and goodwill. In the centre, surrounding the monstrance, a group of priests in their bright white albs, in an attitude of prayer, stand out against the dark shades in the rest of the picture. On the left, devout women in black wearing mantilla shawls are kneeling. Sketched in on the right is a group of rioters looking on expectantly and aggressively as if set on resuming the violence.

The same themes were perfected in composition and execution at a later stage, in works like **The Burial of the Sardine** (*El entierro de la sardine)* and some of the Black Paintings, but Goya set the stage back in his youth at the age of twenty while living in Zaragoza.

The second picture in the series ***is Charles III Issuing the Edict Expelling the Jesuits*** *(Carlos III promulgando el edicto de la expulsión de los jesuitas).* The King is addressing the members of the Council of State to try to resolve the conflict created by the Esquilache Riot which occurred in Madrid and continued in other cities like Zaragoza, as we have seen in the description of the Broqueleros. One of the main consequences of the uprising was the expulsion of the Jesuits from Spain and the replacement of the Neapolitan minister, the Marquis of Esquilache by the Aragonese Count of Aranda.

1768-1769

In the ***Apparition of the Virgin of the Pillar to Saint James and his Saragossan disciples*** *(Aparición de la Virgen del Pilar a Santiago y sus discípulos zaragozanos),* the religious subject matter, the arrangement of the characters and the overall composition of the picture are also derived from that early reliquary door painting in Fuendetodos. Although this work features the linear strokes Goya had learned with Luzán, there are clear signs of the looser brushwork that would become a hallmark of his later paintings, including those in the *coreto* of the Basilica of El Pilar.

1768-1770

In these years, Goya painted **Rest on the Flight to Egypt** (*Descanso durante la huida a Egipto*), **Lamentation over the Body of Christ** (*Lamentación sobre el cuerpo de Cristo*) and **Mary Crying over Christ's Body** (*María llorando sobre el cuerpo de Cristo*).

1769-1770

The Ecstasy of Saint Anthony Abbot (*El éxtasis de San Antonio Abad*). There are a number of small paintings by Goya on this theme, based on Corrado Giaquinto's work in the Church of San Giovanni Celibita in Rome.

The picture considered to be the earliest of these, owing to its lighter, faster brushwork, belongs to a private collection and was recently discovered by Goya expert Arturo Ansón.

Another, auctioned in late 2020 must have been completed after successive modifications of a sketch made in the Church of San Giovanni.

The third belongs to the Goya Museum collection in Zaragoza and was restored in the Prado Museum in 2017 and attributed to Goya.

In all of them, the saint is sitting on a rock looking up in ecstasy at an angel whose left hand is pointing heavenwards announcing his forthcoming death. The colours evoke dusk, with dark green trees in the background landscape, on the ground lie a cross, a book, a pitcher, and other symbols of the saint's ascetic life of prayer.

1770

The Italian Sketchbook appeared at the 1993 exhibition at the Prado Museum "Goya, Fantasy and Invention." Begun on his trip to Italy, the book contains very diverse information, and is a kind of disorderly diary about the artist's work, which deals with personal, economic, and artistic matters.

Particularly noteworthy are his Vatican works, including the Belvedere Torso and the Farnese Hercules, the Genesis fresco in the Sistine Chapel and the preparatory work for Hannibal, Saint Barbara, the Death of Saint Francis Xavier, the Virgin of the Pillar, and his early sketches for the murals in the Aula Dei Charterhouse.

The notebook also suggests Goya's multifaceted and sometimes enigmatic character, expressed in many drawings and disconnected notes, interspersed with the outlines of donkeys, cats, masks and instruments, with captions and sayings rather like those he would later use in his etching series. Interestingly, there are no portraits in the book, even though this was an art in which Goya specialized after his arrival in Madrid and in which he acquired universal fame.

The magnificent composition obtained by combining the many different figures and groups from the series of frescoes in the Chapel of Saint Anthony of La Florida has been compared to the Correggio's paintings in Parma Cathedral, which Goya had chance to see during his trip to Italy. But although the composition is similar, Goya's own hand is clearly visible in the brushwork, light and colours.

One of the first portraits Goya painted was ***Manuel de Vargas Machuca***. The subject was an architect and a disciple of Ventura Rodríguez. Machuca's projects were awarded first prize by the San Fernando Royal Academy.

The Flight to Egypt *(La huida a Egipto)* is Goya's first known print. The plate was etched in 1771. Its lines are simple with more focus on the application of the new technique than on the expression of the figures or elements of the work, all of which are unnatural and with an abundance of the Neoclassical linearity Goya used at the time — a result of his time at the Luzán Academy and his contact with Bayeu.

Clearly influenced by Giambattista and Giovanni Domenico Tiépolo, this aquatint, followed in 1775 by the more successful ***Saint Isidore and Saint Francis of Paola,*** marks the start of Goya's vast work in this field, which would continue with ***Los Caprichos, The Disasters of War, Tauromaquia and The Follies or Proverbs,*** and conclude with the lithographs of ***The Bulls of Bordeaux,*** in his final years.

Goya's first works on the subject of classical mythology were:

*The **Victorious Hannibal Seeing Italy from the Alps for the First Time*** *(Aníbal vencedor que desde lo alto de los Alpes contempla por primera vez Italia),* ***Sacrifice to Vesta*** *(Sacrificio a Vesta),* ***Sacrifice to Pan*** *(Sacrificio a Pan),* ***The Feast of Esther and Ahasuerus*** *(El festín de Ester y Asier), El perdón de Amán,* and ***Venus and Adonis***. These were executed on his trip to Italy, and he inserts monuments and sculptures of Antiquity into the paintings.

In ***Hannibal,*** two aspects in particular will have surprised the Parma Academy jury, namely Goya's treatment of light — with his wide range of delicate hues and chiaroscuro — and his loose brushwork on the groups of figures and landscapes accompanying the main character, in an explosion of Giaquinto-style rococo. This will have been quite different from what was being taught and followed at the Parma Academy, which may well have been a factor in Goya's failure to win first prize. Although the judges acknowledged the merit of the work, they justified their decision on the basis that it had failed to comply with competition rules and that the delicate shades used were inappropriate for a warrior. First prize went to Paolo Borroni's very dark painting where the figure of Hannibal undoubtedly lacks the strength and grandeur of Goya's hero. A sketch drawn in sanguine can be found in his Italian Sketchbook.

1771-1772

On his return from Italy, Goya was commissioned on 21 October 1771 to paint the fresco ***The Adoration of the Name of God*** *(La Adoración del nombre de Dios)* for the *coreto* of the Basilica of El Pilar, opposite the Holy Chapel, which he finished in 1772. This work augurs the sketchy brushwork that would characterize many of Goya's subsequent works and depicts the Trinity worshipped by the angels as it descends to earth, in soft colours and with magnificent perspective. There are three preparatory drawings for this: ***Sketch, drawing for the head of an angel*** and ***Drawing for the head of a forward-facing angel.***

At the same time, Goya also produced oil paintings for the Palace of the Count of Gabarda or Sobradiel, in Zaragoza, as we shall see below. Here we see his Italian influence, especially that of Corregio, whose work he had seen during his stay in Italy.

- ***Saint Joseph's Dream*** *(El sueño de San José).* This oil painting on the oratory wall (right side) was passed to canvas in 1915 at the behest of its owner Joaquín Cavero y Fichar, the Count of Gabarda. It is painted in Baroque style with special emphasis on both the real and spiritual light emanating from above, and the soft colours defining Saint Joseph's cape with masterly brushstrokes which blend the figure and the angel's wings to such an extent that they become one with the space around them. The Virgin Mary can also be seen as a clear but discreetly sketched figure in the background.

- ***The Visitation*** (*La visitación*) painted on the left wall
- ***The Burial of Christ*** *(El entierro de Cristo)* on the ceiling
- ***Saint Anne, Saint Joachim, Saint Vincent Ferrer*** and ***Saint Cajetan*** are painted opposite, facing the altar. Saint Cajetan was painted in honour of the square (Plaza de San Cayetano) on which the palace stood.

1771-1774

In ***The Death of Saint Francis Xavier*** *(La muerte de San Francisco Javier)* the saint is on his deathbed, clutching a crucifix and lying beneath a canopy of branches on Shangchuan Island. Above him are two angels, and the Portuguese ships can be seen setting off across the ocean. The colours are restrained with light effects accentuating the serenity of the saint's demeanour which Goya has executed with meticulous attention to detail. It would have been painted for the purposes of family devotion.

The Virgin of the Pillar is currently in the Museum of Zaragoza. Our Lady of the Pillar is once again the subject of this painting, although here Goya has dispensed with other figures to focus on the Virgin alone who appears resplendent among clouds and angels. This attention to her figure, and the detailed portrayal of her cloak and the child in a picture where other characters are depicted with sketchy brushwork suggest it was intended for private worship and devotion.

1771-1775

The Baptism of Christ *(El Bautismo de Cristo)* is one of the biblical themes that appears in the Italian Sketchbook and was commissioned by Goya's friend Juan Martín de Goicoechea. The composition of the figures was later used in other works like ***The Fight at the Cock Inn /Brawl at the Mesón del Gallo Inn*** *(La riña en el Mesón del Gallo).*

The *Self-Portrait* painted in these years is considered Goya's first. The face is realistic and finished in Mengs's style on an undeveloped bust. A little over twenty, the painter has a firm, searching gaze and a serious, rather sardonic expression, both sensual and intelligent. It is an image to which Goya will return in later paintings like ***The Sermon of Saint Bernardine of Siena*** *(La predicación de San Bernardino de Siena)*, in the Royal Basilica of Saint Francis the Great in Madrid.

1772

Goya painted the Holy Fathers of the Church on the pendentives of the Chapel of Nuestra Señora de la Fuente in Muel, a village near Fuendetodos

He also painted the four Church Fathers in Remolinos, this time in oval shapes on the pendentives in the parish church. In this case, however, Saint Gregory appears in forms and contrasts that are clearly Baroque in style. Goya's school friend from Zaragoza, Nicolás Barta, was instrumental in the commissioning of this work.

1773

Portrait presumed to be the artist, ***Portrait of a Man with a Hat*** *(Cabeza de hombre con sombrero)*, depicted on the front cover, although it has been attributed to Goya, there is doubt as to whether the painter and man depicted is actually Goya or rather Francisco Bayeu. This finished sketch shows the head of man covered in an elegant hat — more in Bayeu's style — whose direct and expressive face is slimmer, with a finer nose and ear than the man featured in Goya's first self-portrait.

1774

The authorship of the portrait of ***The Count of Miranda*** *(El Conde de Miranda)* is in dispute, and could be either by Goya or by Mengs, although Camón Aznar attributes it to Goya. The name of the sitter and the year appear on the handle of his stick.

In 1774, his final year in Zaragoza, Goya finished the fresco murals on the ***Life of the Virgin*** in the Aula Dei Charterhouse, which he painted in a dignified, formal Neoclassical style. The experience of using a large mural space into which he fitted scenes featuring people, groups and diverse landscape was essential for Goya, as it assisted him when he came to tackle his first assignments — the tapestry cartoons — in Madrid.

A few kilometres from the city of Zaragoza, the Charterhouse of Aula Dei was awarded cultural heritage status in 2012 when the Carthesian monks handed it over to the Chemin Neuf religious community to take in families, with or without children, and people who wished to follow Christian training courses. In 2019, it had 120 residents of 19 different nationalities, 30 of whom were children at the public-sector school in the nearby village of San Mateo de Gállego. That same year, thousands of people came to see the Goya paintings on show there.

These include a monumental series of eleven mural frescoes on the life of the Virgin Mary and the Christ Child painted on the walls of the church. Of these, seven original paintings are fully preserved: ***Portico of Saint Joachim and Saint Anne, Marriage of the Virgin, Birth of the Virgin, The Visitation, The Adoration of the Magi, The Circumcision*** and ***The Presentation in the Temple.***

After 1775, Madrid and Aragón

During his first years in Madrid, Goya stayed in close contact with Zaragozan friends, who helped him settle into Madrid society, obtain commissions for paintings, and meet important figures with connections to the Royal Court.

His friend and protector Juan Martín de Goicoechea y Gabarza, was the Zaragozan representative of the National San Carlos Bank, founded in 1782, by a Royal Decree of Graces, issued by Charles III. Goicoechea put him in contact with the bank's secretary Ceán Bermúdez, whose wife María Margarita Camas was also from Aragón. As a result, Goya became the bank's portrait artist and responsible for painting its managers. Ceán Bermúdez was also secretary to Minister Gaspar Melchor de Jovellanos. These clients and acquaintances brought Goya into contact with the Enlightenment ideology of the day, which he himself came to share. He was particularly close to Jovellanos. They both attended the Campomanes salon which was frequented by leading figures in the worlds of art, politics, and economics. They were also neighbours in Calle Carrera de San Jerónimo and became members of the San Fernando Royal Academy of Fine Arts in the same year, 1780.

Goya met Infante Luis of Bourbon and his Zaragozan wife María Teresa de Vallabriga through his brother-in-law Vicente Marcos del Campo, who worked for him and was married to Josefa's younger sister María Bayeu. In 1783, he was invited to their palace in Arenas de San Pedro, and during his stay painted the magnificent ***The Family of the Infante, Don Luis*** (*La familia del Infante D. Luis de Borbón*). He later painted portraits of their children. Particularly outstanding is the picture of their daughter ***The Countess of Chinchón,*** pregnant with her first child by her husband, the Prime Minister Manuel Godoy.

Goya met the royal family when he was painting the portraits of the Aragonese magistrate, ***José de Cistué y Coll***, ***Baron of La Menglana*** who married María Josefa Martínez, chamber maid to María Luisa of Parma, and that of his son ***Luis María de Cistué y Martínez***, whom he immortalized in a memorable portrait just before the little boy turned three. Charles IV, the Prince of Asturias, and his fiancée María Luisa had been godparents at the child's christening.

He also painted ***Joaquina Candado Ricarte***, a widow from Zaragoza. Her second husband was paymaster at the Royal Saltpeter factory, as a result of which she came to live in Madrid, where she forged important friendships with people including the Duchess of Osuna, whose Enlightenment ideas she shared. In 2017, the historian Julián Vidal analysed X-rays of the portrait and confirmed two sketches underneath. The first was the ***Immaculate Conception***, which had been on the altar of the chapel on the canal by the Jalón River aqueduct and today is part of a private collection; the second was of the young Vicente Osorio, eldest son of the Duke and Duchess of Osuna.

Goya's friendship with Ramón de Pignatelli, promoter of Aragon's Imperial Canal, led to commissions for a number of religious paintings for canal facilities and for the new Church of San Fernando de Torrero. Goya produced three large paintings described by Jovellanos, on his trip to Zaragoza in 1801, as "admirable works, not only in their composition, but for the power of their chiaroscuro, the peerless beauty of their colour and a certain magic in their lights and pigments, which appear to be out of the reach of any other brush." Only the preparatory drawings for these works are known, as the originals disappeared during the Napoleonic invasion. To date, a Royal Order of 1814 calling on France to restore "all the papers, paintings and objects of Fine Art and Natural History that were transferred to that Kingdom by the intruder government of Joseph Bonaparte" has gone unheeded.

In Madrid, Goya stayed in contact with the members of the Zaragoza drawing academy where he had been a pupil, sending material for use in class and keeping them up to date on the latest techniques in painting, sculpture, printmaking, and architecture. He also hosted young artists from the academy who came to Madrid to perfect their skills. In gratitude for his support and the part he had played in the school's new status as San Luis Royal Academy of Noble and Fine Arts, he was appointed Distinguished Academician in 1796 when he was court painter to King Charles IV.

However, one of his compatriots whom Goya never painted was Pedro Pablo de Bolea y Ximénez de Urrea, the Count of Aranda, despite his serving in different eminent positions, including Captain General, ambassador and prime minister under Philip V, Ferdinand VI, Charles III and Charles IV. A strong character like Goya, Charles IV described the Count as "more stubborn and obstinate than an Aragonese mule." The two men had mutual friends among royalty and senior members of the military, clergy, and entrepreneurs of their day, but the rift between them may have had a number of causes:

- Although both came from small villages in Aragón, the Count of Aranda was of noble blood and his family owned a major ceramic factory in Alcora, whereas Goya's family were middle class.
- The Count received a select and elite education with the Jesuits in Zaragoza, and at the age of nine his father enrolled him in the Parma Academy of Nobility in Italy, from where he went on to a brilliant military, diplomatic and political career. By contrast, Goya went to the public school in Fuendetodos until he was thirteen, before attending the Piarists School in Zaragoza and Luzán's drawing academy.
- Goya was involved in the Broqueleros Riots in Zaragoza in 1766, which the Count had repressed with extreme force, leading Goya to take refuge in Calatayud.
- The Count of Aranda's daughter had married the eldest son of the Count of Fuentes, José María de Pignatelli, who allegedly had a relationship with the actress María Ladvenant whom the Count had expelled from Zaragoza after one of her performances ended in scandal. Goya shared Pignatelli's admiration for and friendship with the actress whose portrait he painted on two occasions.
- The Count failed to use his political influence when Grimaldi was Secretary of State and enacted the Pragmatic Sanction which affected the morganatic marriage of the Infante Don Luis and his Aragonese wife María Teresa de Vallabriga. The family, who were friends of Goya's, were forced to leave Madrid for Arenas de San Pedro where Goya painted them on several occasions.

The Count therefore showed little interest in the painter, despite their common roots in Aragón. And Goya, with his genius and determination, went on to paint the portraits of other eminent figures, leaving the Count out of his portfolio.

Chapter 8

Love and Friendship, Liaisons, and Low Life

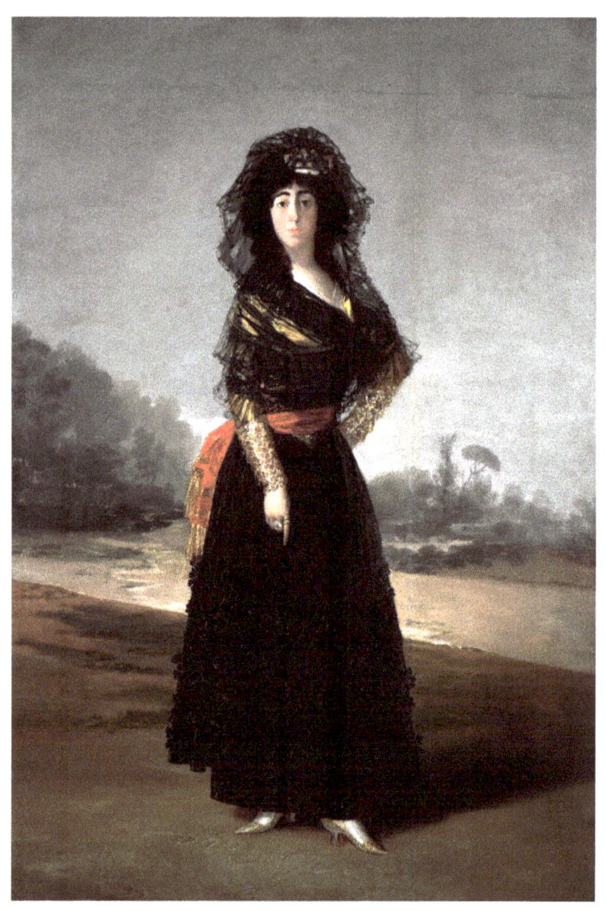

The Duchess of Alba. Spanish Society. New York.

Love

Goya's love and affection for his family is no secret. He lived with his parents throughout his childhood and youth, then cared for them in their old age, showing his regard and respect until the end of their lives. Goya painted a subdued and dignified portrait of his mother, her head held high, and her white hair pulled back from her face. She is wearing a simple, but elegant Aragonese costume, with its typical skirt, headdress, and blouse in different shades of grey, and holding a rosary in her hands. Further evidence of Goya's sense of duty to his parents is his rejection of the offer to take up a position with the Empress at the Russian court, choosing instead to stay close to his family and continue to support them, both economically and personally, as they largely depended on him.

He also helped his brothers and sister, sending money via his friend Martín Zapater, when they were living with his mother in Zaragoza. He supervised his younger brother's career in the Church and was responsible for the Infante Luis of Spain's appointment of Camilo to the position of parish priest of Chinchón, where Luis was Lord. Goya helped his brother Tomás find work as a gilder in Zaragoza and later Madrid, and then bought him a farmstead in Fuendetodos, where he settled with his wife and two children. Their descendants continued to live in Fuendetodos until quite recently.

Goya depicts his wife, showing signs of age and fatigue, in one honest portrait of Josefa. He took her on trips to Valencia when she was ill or in low spirits and, in his correspondence with Martín Zapater, lamented her illnesses and the hardships of childbirth she had to endure. The couple had to suffer the tragic death of six of their seven children at an early age. "Pepa has given birth, thank God, to a very handsome boy", he wrote on one occasion. A devout Christian, Josefa venerated Our Lady of the Pillar, and presented a blue cape, intricately embroidered in gold, to adorn the image in the Basilica. She died in 1812 at the age of 65.

Goya was particularly dedicated and affectionate to his only surviving son Javier, whom he portrayed in elegant dress in ***Javier Goya Bayeu***, and to his grandson, who featured in a number of pictures, including one as a child in 1814, ***Mariano Goya Goicoechea.*** Here, with an innocent but aristocratic look, the young boy is dressed like a gentleman, wearing a stylish black top hat with wisps of blond hair peeking out, and has a piece of music in front of him.

Once a widower, in the final years of his life, Goya lived with Leocadia Weis and her young daughter María del Rosario in the *Quinta del Sordo* villa. They then accompanied him into exile in Bordeaux until his death. He became godfather to María, whom he took under his wing, teaching her to paint. She later became a member of the San Fernando Royal Academy of Fine Arts and a drawing teacher to the Spanish Infantas.

Friendship

As we have seen throughout the book, Goya forged friendships with people from all social classes. With his natural empathy, he made long-lasting bonds at school and at the drawing academy in Zaragoza. He also befriended people from all walks of life, from royalty, the aristocracy, the military, the clergy, and politicians to actresses, bullfighters, and writers, many of whom appear in his portraits.

In Zaragoza, his first friendships at the drawing academy brought him into contact with a wide group of young people who met to socialize in a room in Martín Zapater y Clavería's house. They included Antonio Grasa, a farmer; Manuel de Yoldy, a scribe at the main law court in Aragón; Alejandro Ortiz, a medical student who would go on to become a professor at the University of Zaragoza; Tomás Pallas, a student at the Military Academy, and Francisco Javier Pirán, who was an accountant in the offices of the Imperial Canal and was later a representative once Zapater had become a well-known businessman in Madrid. He acted as middleman in many of the commissions that passed between them.

Goya and his friends sometimes organized raucous night jaunts around the taverns of Zaragoza where wine and spirits flowed freely, *tiranas* and *seguidillas* were danced, and *jota* folk songs were improvised. On one such nocturnal visit to Zaragoza, after he had moved to Madrid, Goya told his friend Grasa to go into La Mariquita tavern in Calle de Carbonero and inform the innkeeper that he had come on behalf of the painter from Fuendetodos who daubed his walls and tables as a younger man, to pay back a debt of twenty *reales* — quite a large sum at the time, equivalent to five days' wages for a master builder — and to pick up a portrait for his mother which he had left there as a pledge. In a letter to Zapater in 1781, a 35-year-old Goya recalled those nights on the town in playful tone: "You and I have been such rogues, we had better make amends in the time that is left to us."

Goya's friendship with Zapater was undoubtedly the longest and most intense for much of his life. Zapater came from a well-off Zaragozan family of upper middle-class merchants. He had important business dealings in Madrid and in 1789 the king made him Nobleman of Aragón in recognition of his generous donations of wheat and money to the Council of Zaragoza in times of food shortage. Goya, from a more modest background, was keen to keep his friend abreast of his social ascent and shared with him his satisfaction when he had his first audience with the royal family.

The friendship dated back to the years when the boys were at the Piarist School, a period they recalled in their correspondence as they grew older, and Goya moved to Madrid in 1775. By 1799, four years before the death of the unmarried Zapater, Goya had written 147 letters, focusing on their days together in Zaragoza. Goya makes no mention of his childhood in Fuendetodos, which was before the boys met. Perhaps he considered that village life would in any case be of little interest to wealthier members of Zaragozan society.

The language used in their correspondence is typical of the teenage years they had shared. Spontaneous, intimate, and familiar, there is no pomp or ceremony, and their colloquialisms include popular Aragonese expressions of their day. Their complicity is reflected in the coarse vocabulary and sometimes bawdy tone used in Goya's very male jokes about sex and dalliances with women, accompanied by lewd pictures recalling wild nights out in Zaragozan taverns. These memories, and in the belief that Goya perhaps continued to let off steam in the same way, Zapater — once he himself was an upright citizen —seems to have suggested in a letter to another friend that the severe illness plaguing Goya which turned him permanently deaf might be a consequence of his "dissolute lifestyle."

The two friends shared tastes, interests, and sorrows. At Christmas, Goya asked Zapater to buy him *turrón* almond sweets and *anguilas,* marzipan sweetmeats made in the shape of an eel and filled with a squash preserve called *cabello de ángel.* Zapater ordered fabric from Madrid for his aunts, which Goya's wife Josefa would then buy for him in the capital. Both men were fond of luxury and commented on their purchases of expensive dresses and new vehicles like Goya's hansom cab. They shared the joy of the birth of the Goyas' children and sadness when Josefa fell ill, and their children died. Zapater kept Goya up to date with news of his family in Zaragoza and took them money to facilitate their day-to-day lives.

Perhaps there was little room for politics or conflict in this private and affectionate correspondence. Indeed, Goya made just a single reference to the British ships captured by the Spanish Armada, and another to the Treaty of Versailles of 1783 when Spain recognized the independence of British colonies in the Americas and recovered Menorca.

However, it is possible that one of the reasons for the end of their communication in 1801 may have been Zapater's position in favour of the war against the French Republic, which was opposed by many Enlightenment advocates.

Surprisingly, the introduction and presentation to Volume II of the Prado's new *catalogue raisonné* in December 2018 suggests the relationship between Goya and Zapater may have been a homosexual one, with reference to the rather affected phrase *"amitié amoureuse."* The evidence given revolves around a letter signed by his wife Josefa and a group of friends who had gathered at Goya's house, sent to Zapater in December 1790.

The letter includes a scatological drawing of a man — although some historians like Mercedes Águeda and Xavier de Salas (2003) believe it to be a woman — kneeling on a cushion with naked buttocks facing the reader. The text of the letter suggests it was written during an animated tea party which was well supplied with food and drink sent from Aragón by Zapater himself to his friends in Madrid, to celebrate winning the lottery. The atmosphere may well have been raucous and the party in full swing when, as the letter describes, wine glasses flew and were shattered on the ground after drinking a toast. The picture in question may have been a result of those circumstances and is insufficient to determine that Goya was homosexual.

In the same context, we should remember that Goya's wife Josefa became pregnant twenty times and that, once widowed, Goya lived with Leocadia Weis, mother of a child whose paternity is indeed sometimes attributed to him. This, coupled with his many purported affairs with actresses and portrait sitters, would appear to make homosexuality improbable.

The friendship between Goya and Zapater was undoubtedly a close and loving one, albeit not in the manner suggested in the catalogue. Friendship can take multiple forms and has been defined in many ways throughout history by writers and philosophers. William Penn, for instance, described it the union of spirits and a marriage of hearts (1693), whilst Silvio Pellico saw it as a fraternal relationship and, in its highest sense, the most beautiful ideal of brotherhood (1834).

The writer Antonio Peiró Arroyo, author of a book published this year entitled *Martín Zapater. Amigo de Goya y noble de Aragón,* states that Martín Zapater's inclination for women is in any case well documented and that many writers have let their imaginations run riot on the subject of the friendship between the two men.

Zapater corresponded with many friends other than Goya, including the Piarist Father Joaquín and the manager of the San Carlos Bank, Francisco Cabarrús. But sadly, none of the many letters he undoubtedly wrote to Goya have been found, preventing us from seeing his own perspective on important aspects of their friendship.

After he moved to Madrid, Goya stayed in contact with his Zaragozan friends. He kept Martín Goicoechea informed about new pictorial and architectural styles emerging and sent drawings from the San Fernando Academy to students at the academy in Zaragoza. He also sent letters of recommendation to eminent members of the clergy at the Basilica of El Pilar, who worked with the San Luis Academy, seeking support for young painters and sculptors from Aragón who came to Madrid to perfect their technique, such as Latassa and Ponzano.

He was instrumental in Charles IV's decision to allow the San Luis Academy of Fine Arts to incorporate the word 'royal' into its title, in a decree of 1792 put forward by the Count of Aranda. In recognition of his ongoing support for the institution and its students, Goya was made a Distinguished Academician in 1796.

Goya was also friends with bullfighters like the highly popular Pedro Romero, who invited him to *capeas* with smaller bulls, in one of which, ***La novillada***, Goya, as we have seen above, included a self-portrait.

Goya had a long-standing friendship with the Pignatellis, a powerful aristocratic family for whom he showed respect and appreciation all his life. He met the 16th Count of Fuentes and Lord of Fuendetodos, Atanasio Pignatelli of Aragón, on one of his visits to Fuendetodos while still a child, and later in his palace in Zaragoza, opposite the Goyas' house in Calle de la Morería Cerrada. He knew Vicente, a priest, painter, and patron of the Zaragoza Drawing Academy. His brother José, a Jesuit who was later made a saint, was Goya's grammar teacher in Zaragoza, and he also visited him on his trip to Italy, as we have seen. Goya had dealings with brother Ramón, a canon and promoter of the Imperial Canal of Aragón and the San Luis Academy of Fine Arts on many occasions and produced a striking portrait of him on one of his stays in Zaragoza. José María, the Count's eldest son, died at the age of just 34. He was married to the Count of Aranda's daughter, and Goya had met him in his youth in

Zaragoza. The two men went to the playhouse together and shared an appreciation for the actresses who performed there.

Cayetana, Duchess of Alba

Cayetana's mother Mariana, the sister of the Marquis of Santa Cruz, married the Duke of Alba Francisco de Paula de Silva y Álvarez de Toledo, in 1757, and their only child, Cayetana, was born in 1762, becoming the Duchess of Alba at the age of just eight when her father died in 1770.

In 1775, the widowed Mariana married her second husband, the 16th Count of Fuentes and Lord of Fuendetodos, making the Count of Fuentes Cayetana's stepfather when she was thirteen.

Goya was also friends with the Marquis and Marchioness of Santa Cruz, who frequently visited Mariana's family. In 1781, at the age of 47, the 9th Marquis of Santa Cruz de Mudela, José Joaquín Silva Bazán, Cayetana's uncle, married his second wife the Austrian aristocrat **Marianne Waldstein** aged eighteen, when his niece Cayetana was nineteen. Goya painted a full-length picture of Marianne wearing an intricate black lace *mantilla* shawl, in 1797.

Goya undoubtedly had a special friendship with the Duchess of Alba. It was the relationship of an artist sixteen years her senior and from a very different social background, with a beautiful young aristocrat and leading figure in Madrid's social life. Capricious and unpredictable, she protected the painter and showed her affection towards him, which he returned by painting delightful portraits and drawings of scenes from her private family life in Sanlúcar de Barrameda. The relationship was almost one of kinship, as Goya was well acquainted with her mother Mariana, the

Marquis and Marchioness of Santa Cruz and her stepfather the Count of Fuentes.

He paints Cayetana as tall, slim and elegant, distant, serious and with a haughty expression. On the death of her husband, ***José Álvarez de Toledo, Duque de Alba,*** in 1796, the Duchess of Alba, aged 34, retired to Sanlúcar de Barrameda where she was visited by Goya, who painted the magnificent ***Cayetana de Silva Alvarez de Toledo, 13th Duchess of Alba***, in a traditional black dress in the *maja* style, with lace, *mantilla* and two rings on her right hand bearing the names Goya and Alba, pointing to an inscription in the sand which reads "Only Goya. 1797." During his stay, Goya produced a number of drawings of the Duchess's simple, everyday life.

Contrary to some claims, the Duchess of Alba is not the young woman in the two paintings ***The Naked Maja*** and ***The Clothed Maja***. As an old man, Goya's grandson, Mariano claimed the model was actually a young woman who had been abandoned when she was gravely ill and was then saved from death by a friar acquainted with Goya.

Indeed, the *maja*'s physique and firm, bright skin suggests a woman who was younger, plumper, and shorter than the older, taller Duchess. Goya painted these pictures in 1800, when the Duchess was 38, just two years before she died, making it unlikely she was the sitter for these portraits. The Aragonese writer Ramón J. Sender had this to say on the subject:

> The Clothed and Naked *Majas* have given rise to much popular fantasy. These portraits have been linked to the Duchess of Alba, even though in another of the painter's portraits of the Duchess, wearing a black *mantilla*, the Duchess is tall, whereas the *Majas*, both clothed and naked, are small and doll-like, although very well proportioned. The short thigh of

the *maja* does not match that of the Duchess as painted in the portrait where she is standing.

Other writers like Günter Kunert have referred to the *maja's* vitality:

Goya also had a close friendship with María Teresa de Vallabriga. Born in Zaragoza, she was married to Infante Luis of Bourbon, Charles III's brother. Luis's marriage was declared morganatic, and when banished from court, the couple went to live in their palaces in Arenas de San Pedro and Boadilla del Monte. In the Infante's service was Marcos del Campo who married the younger sister of Goya's wife Josefa Bayeu in the same year Goya visited them in Arenas de San Pedro.

In about 1783, Goya produced a memorable portrait of the Infante and his family in which, recalling Velázquez's Meninas, he painted himself into the picture, though with his back to the viewers. Thus, he puts the spotlight on the scene where the family and their servants are gathered around the Infantes during a game of cards, while the Infanta is having her hair done. Also featured are their son Luis — whom Goya painted as an adolescent and later as cardinal and advisor to the parliament at the Cádiz *Cortes* — and their daughter María Teresa, whom he had also painted as a girl.

Another memorable portrait, painted in 1800, features María Teresa de Borbón y Vallabriga in the portrait ***The Countess of Chinchón***, when pregnant by her husband Manuel Godoy. The picture captures her sense of melancholy and resignation, her head crowned with ears of corn representing the future life towards which she appears to be gazing, her hand protecting her belly as if hoping the child she is expecting will be born into a new world.

The poet María Victoria Atencia dedicated a poem to the Countess of Chinchón, conjuring up the sweet sense of melancholy of impending motherhood:

> To break the silence, withered ears of corn
> brush against an angel passing through your red curls
> or perhaps because you — who lacked everything —
> have not yet lost your docile, convent-like freshness.
> From a borrowed armchair, you contemplate the
> unfolding comedy
> and, with absent arms, surround the toy
> within a womb used by royal appointment.[28].

Perhaps Goya's last friend was a young milkmaid in Bordeaux who appears in what is considered his final portrait and striking precursor of Impressionism, ***The Milkmaid of Bordeaux***. Goya is said to have practised his French with her and commented on the news in Bordeaux during their daily conversations when she brought the milk each morning.

---

[28] Por romper el silencio, mustias espigas roza
un ángel cuando pasa sobre tus bucles jaros
o porque no has perdido aún —tú, la carente
de todo— una frescura conventual y dócil.
Desde un sillón prestado contemplas la comedia
y, con ausentes brazos, abarcas el juguete
de tu vientre de ocasión por encargos reales

Liaisons

Goya painted what he saw and experienced, and this included coquetry and courtship, and the liaisons between cloaked *majos* and *majas,* dressed in traditional costume enjoying a day on San Isidro meadow, flirting and dancing amorously in the field known as La Bombilla.

He was particularly drawn to female beauty which he expressed so splendidly in his pictures. A fine connoisseur of female psychology, Goya used his empathy and knowledge of his models, which he engaged in conversation as they sat for him, skilfully evoking not only their physical form but delving into their psyche. Their spirits are portrayed through the position of arms and legs, bodily stance, the serious or cheerful expressions on their faces, the goodness or anger in their gaze, the smile or mischief in their eyes, their beauty, and their ugliness.

Though he could sometimes be rough and frank to the point of rudeness, Goya painted many sensitive portraits of women. ***The Pottery Vendor*** (*El Cacherrero*) features a beautiful noblewoman seated in a carriage so that she can visit the fair without being recognised. Men are given the slip in ***Blind Man's Bluff*** *(La gallina ciega),* while in ***The Straw Manikin** (El Pelele)* women are tossing the male doll up high in the air with great amusement. Then there are the many dark-eyed, charming *majas,* like those listening to the madrigals recited by royal guards or the compliments paid by the young men in ***The Maja and the Cloaked Men*** *(La maja y los embozados).*

Goya's drawings often draw on the plays of Ramón de la Cruz, as models of integrity and virtue, and on his farces on comic situations, family dramas and liaisons between men and women.

After watching a bullfight or a comedy, Goya liked to go to the taverns with fellow revellers to drink wine and spirits, dance popular *tiranas* and *seguidillas* and sing folk songs into the wee small hours with the performers, bullfighters and *majos* courting the ladies

Goya's behaviour with family, and with Enlightened, aristocratic, or royal friends and acquaintances clearly differed from those wild nights of his youth. But even these cannot be compared to the attitudes of the more debauched low life of his day, which he depicted critically in his work, particularly his prints, and which he himself profoundly rejected.

Low Life

Many of Goya's drawings are highly critical of the low life and dissolute behaviour of his day, where young women were prostituted by pimps, procuresses, and middlemen.

Prints from **Los Caprichos** and **Los Disparates** (*The Follies*) criticize and denounce the bad habits and vices that abounded in Spain, and which he encountered in both Zaragoza and Madrid. At the time, there were thousands of taverns and brothels where lecherous or naïve customers were fleeced by procurers, prostitutes, dishonest gamblers, and criminals of all kinds, like those featured in **There they go, plucked** (*Ya van desplumados*).

Also plentiful are the fake processions and *romerías* with prostitutes and their go-betweens purporting to be their mothers, as in **It is nicely stretched** (*Bien tirada está*), and picnics and street parties swarming with low life, suitably dressed and disguised to trap the unwary.

Goya denounced the terrible and often painful consequences of such debauchery, depicting young women in jail in **Because she was susceptible** (*Por que fue sensible*), acts of violence against them, diseases that destroyed them, corrupt guards who abused their position, mistreating their prisoners and even torturing them in cruel ways, as in the drawing which bears the caption: ***In Saragossa, in the middle of the last century, they put a constable called Lampiños in the body of a dead nag, and sewed him in; he stayed alive all night.***

Baudelaire (1857) described the horrific panorama Goya painted in *Beacons*:

> Goya, nightmare filled with things unknown,
> Foetuses roasted at witches' sabbaths,
> Old women at the mirror and naked children,
> Neatly adjusting their hose to tempt the demons.[29]

---

[29] Goya, cauchemar plein de choses inconnues,
De foetus qu'on fait cuire au milieu des sabbats,
De vieilles au miroir et d'enfants toutes nues,
Pour tenter les démons ajustant bien leurs bas. (Les Phares) [own trans]

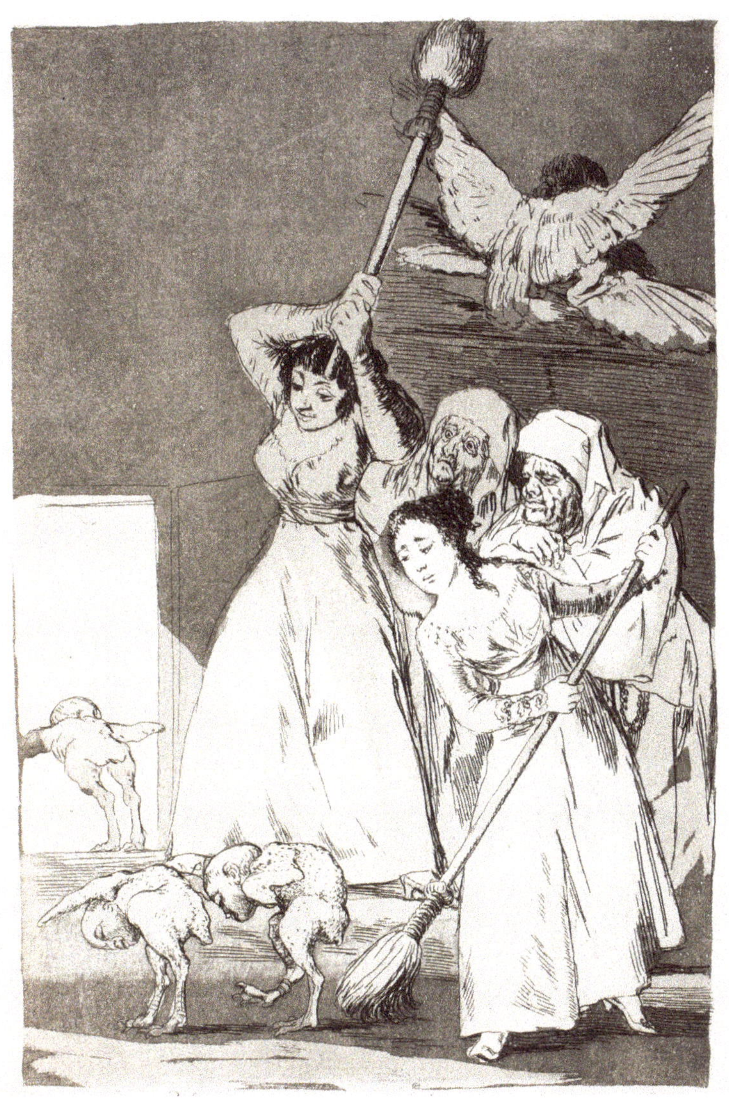

There They Go Plucked.
© Prado Museum Photographic Archive

Chapter 9

Goya and Beethoven

Like the *Parallel Lives* recounted in Plutarch's biographies, Goya's had similarities with those of other geniuses down the ages, some of which, as we shall see, shared his roots in Aragón. We can also draw certain parallels between his life and that of one of his contemporaries, not from Aragón, but from Germany, namely the musical genius Beethoven.

The Spanish word *"rasmia"* has often been used to describe the Aragonese character. Encompassing tenacity, sincerity, loyalty, and creativity in the search for an ideal, it suggests a rough exterior, but someone who is kind and welcoming on the inside. It is a concept that might be applied to many of the Aragonese figures described below.

The poet Marcial was born in 49 A.D. in Augusta Bilbilis in Calatayud, Zaragoza, in Hispania Tarraconensis, and went to Rome at the age of 24 where his epigrams won him the protection of its emperors. In these short verses of Greek origin, Marcial accurately and perceptively described daily life in the society of his day. Like Goya, he appears to have had many loyal friends and when, at the age of 59, he decided to return to an estate in Calatayud he had given to one of them, he wrote a letter praising the virtues of country life, like Goya in his letter to Zapater: "My dear boy, *campicos* are the good life." In one of his epigrams, Marcial too draws parallels between art and nature: "Art, if only you could portray character and soul, no painting on earth would be more beautiful." It was almost a prophecy of what Goya would say and achieve in his pictures, many years later.

Also from Aragón, the tenacious Michael Servetus, born in 1509 in Villanueva de Sigena in Huesca, was burned alive by the Swiss Inquisition in Geneva due to his enmity and religious differences with John Calvin, particularly regarding the existence of the Holy Spirit. He toured all over Europe as part of the household and entourage of Charles V and studied medicine in Paris. His great contribution to the discipline was as the first European to correctly describe the function of pulmonary circulation.

Baltasar Gracián was born in 1601 in Belmonte, a village near Calatayud in the province of Zaragoza. A Jesuit, his work caused him serious problems with the church hierarchy, which condemned Gracián's approach to the Christian soul and its importance for human redemption. Forced to abandon his place of residence and his teaching career on many occasions, he was confined to his cell in Graus on a diet of bread and water. Nonetheless, his iron will, intellectual prowess and fight for freedom to express his philosophical opinions led to the creation of his masterpiece, *El Criticón (The Critic)*. In the search for the perfect man, the novel describes and criticizes mundane vices in a sharp and caustic philosophical account of the rise and triumph of an upright individual without refinement or experience, in a world conditioned by the cunning wickedness of the sophisticated and educated society of his day.

Goya became acquainted with Gracián's ideas in the Madrid salons organized in the homes of enlightened liberal and conservative intellectuals and aristocrats, where the work of well-known artists and writers were discussed in depth in a carefree setting. Gracián undoubtedly embodied the Aragonese character, combining a stubborn attitude with good sense.

Santiago Ramón y Cajal was born in Petilla de Aragón in 1852 and spent his childhood in several Aragonese villages, as his father was a rural doctor. He too studied at a Piarist School, in his case in Jaca, before going on to complete his baccalaureate in Huesca. At the age of sixteen, he studied anatomy, drawing on his father's knowledge and experience. He was also an extremely gifted artist and his magnificent drawings of human anatomy, and the brain were fundamental in his discoveries and teaching. Ramón y Cajal was also in contact with students of the *Institución Libre de Enseñanza*, an educational project which defended human rights and evolutionism. He studied Medicine in Zaragoza and graduated in 1873, at the age of 21, travelling to Cuba as a ship's doctor the following year and returning in 1875 suffering from malaria. He survived serious illness and went to work at Hospital de Gracia in Zaragoza, completed his doctorate and joined a masonic lodge before marrying Gracia Fañanás in 1879, with whom he had seven children, two of whom died in childhood. As Professor of Histology in Barcelona, in 1879 he discovered the processes connecting the nerve cells in the brain and his findings were ratified at the Congress of the German Anatomical Society in 1889. In 1892, he became professor at the Central University of Madrid and was appointed senator by the liberal Catholic and anticlerical Canalejas, who was prime minister in the reign of Alfonso XIII. Cajal was awarded honorary doctorates by many universities and in 1906 won the Nobel Prize in Physiology or Medicine. In retirement, he worked at the Cajal Institute until he died in 1934.

But when considering parallel lives,[30] perhaps one of the figures with most similarities to Goya was a contemporary, though not in this case from Aragón, but from Bonn in Germany, namely the German composer Ludwig van Beethoven. We shall go on to consider what these two men had in common.

Contemporaries, they shared a period in history which for Goya ran from 1746, when he was born in Fuendetodos, until his death in Bordeaux in 1828. Beethoven was born somewhat later in 1770 in Bonn but died at a younger age in Vienna in 1827. From similar middle-class backgrounds in Western Europe, they were initially remote from the spheres of power

---

[30] Luis Carazo. Vidas paralelas. Tras las huellas de Plutarco. Pensamientos y recuerdos. Bonn 2002.

and the dominant classes of their respective countries, run by aristocrats, senior members of the clergy and nobility, major landowners, prominent merchants, and other professionals with connections.

Goya's paternal ancestors were stone masons, as we saw in Chapter 3, who probably travelled to the towns and villages along the Pilgrims Way of Saint James leading to Santiago, like hundreds of other European families at that time. Some would have settled in Spain. When Goya was born in Fuendetodos in 1746, his father was working as a gilder in Zaragoza. On the maternal side, the Lucientes family were farmers, although they spent long periods in the city of Zaragoza.

The name Beethoven is thought to be derived from beet growing, and he was also the great grandson of farmers, in his case from the Flemish region of Brabant, which was part of the Burgundian Netherlands from 1430 to 1482, the Spanish Netherlands from 1482 to 1581 and the Austrian Netherlands from 1581 to 1795. From there, his family moved to Bonn in 1733, a city that was part of the Archdiocese of Cologne and the place where Ludwig was born. His grandfather was a teacher and his father a court tenor. Beethoven moved to Vienna in 1792.

To judge from their portraits, both men had large heads, prominent foreheads, and a similar style of frown. They are depicted with dishevelled hair, bushy eyebrows, a sharp, insightful gaze, and a determined expression with tightly clenched lips. With broad necks and of plump, small stature, they also had dark complexions to the extent that Beethoven's compatriots were known to have referred to him as "the Spanish boy."

Tenacious and energetic, both fitted the Aragonese concept of *rasmia*, and were known for their drive and determination to complete a task. Only thus could they have overcome serious physical disabilities to pursue their art single-mindedly, producing some of their greatest masterpieces at the end of their lives, as is the case of Beethoven's choral *Symphony No. 9 in D minor* of 1824 and Goya's Bordeaux lithographs.

Both men had a limited education. Goya attended the Boys' School in Fuendetodos until the age of thirteen but was able to continue briefly at the Piarist School in Zaragoza, before leaving to become a painter's apprentice at José Luzán's academy. A child prodigy, Beethoven gave a concert in Cologne at the tender age of seven. His father forced him to leave school to devote his energies entirely to music.

Goya's artistic career began at the age of sixteen when he painted the doors of the reliquary in Fuendetodos church. Beethoven published his first composition entitled *Nine variations on a march by Ernst Christoph Dressier (WoO63)* at the age of eleven.

Both geniuses were recognized by royalty and distinguished figures in high-level institutions in Spain and Austria who became their patrons and protectors. Goya was appointed court painter by Charles IV of Spain in 1799, at the age of 53, and with an annuity of 50,000 *reales* a year and over 500 *escudos* for a carriage, which were confirmed in his retirement in Bordeaux. In a letter of 1785, Goya wrote to his friend Zapater: "I always work with the same honour, which is a great pleasure, without having to deal with enemies or be tied down. I do not have to campaign in antechambers; I already have enough to do and have no need to get myself into trouble." And Goya prized his freedom of expression, as is apparent in **Los Caprichos** and **Los Disparates** where he fiercely criticized the vices and shortcomings of the society of his day, from the aristocracy to the clergy, military, and every level of power, not forgetting the common people.

Beethoven was protected by Prince Lichnowsky and the princes of Vienna who supported him financially on condition he remain in the city. In 1809, when he was 39, they settled an annuity of 4,000 florins on him and gave him the freedom to choose his own compositions. Freedom of expression was vital to Beethoven, but a scarce commodity at a time when patrons preferred to stipulate which themes they wished to be composed. Beethoven was a revolutionary and has been considered democracy's first free composer. The Austrian Count Ferdinand Ernst von Waldstein-Wartenberg was Beethoven's patron and paid for two trips to Vienna to continue his musical training. Beethoven repaid the Count with the magnificent Waldstein piano sonata. The Count's younger sister married the 9th Marquis of Santa Cruz when he was widowed, and Goya painted her portrait *Marianna Waldstein, Marchioness of Santa Cruz.*

Both Goya and Beethoven can be considered artists of and for the people. Their works marked the transition from the Old Regime to the beginning of Romanticism. Goya's early tapestry cartoons reflect the immense variety and colours of the landscape and rural activities, the hustle and bustle of the meadows and countryside festivities, with the courtship of *majas* and cloaked representatives of the people. Beethoven composed sonatas, quartets and symphonies evoking country life, with emotional and pastoral sounds and sensations.

There was also a Spanish element to Beethoven's life in his close friendship with Mariana, daughter of the Spanish *hidalgo* Nicolás Martínez who was in the service of the papal nuncio in Vienna. Through her, the composer was invited to salons which kept him up to date with events in Spain following the Peninsular War against the French, of which Goya had personal experience. Beethoven too experienced the violence of French troops during Napoleon's siege of Vienna and the terror caused by the bombardment. Beethoven also chose a Spanish tutor, Cayetano Anastasio del Río, to educate his nephew Karl.

Part of his Symphony No. 6, "Pastoral" draws on popular Spanish music and songs, particularly *tiranas* and *boleros*. In his *Lieder Verschiedener Volker* (WoO 158/a) or 'Songs of various nationalities' for voice, violin, cello and piano, he evokes the *tiranas* of which Goya was so fond, and even uses Spanish lyrics in the song *"La tirana se embarca"*, also known as "The Little Spanish Tyrant", punning on the name *"Tirana."*

The Tirana embarks
From Cádiz to Marseilles
Caught on the high seas
By a French sloop
Ah Tirana, go back to Spain
Ah Tirana, flee from the rigours
Of the Convention
Yes, yes, you Little Tyrant
Yes, yes, you sly little trickster
Because if they catch you
They'll put your head in the guillotine[31]

---

[31] La tirana se embarca
De Cádiz para Marsella
En alta mar la apresó
Una balandra francesa.
Ay! Tirana retírate a España
Ay! Tirana huye los rigores
Ay! Tirana de la Convención
Sí, sí, Tiranilla
Sí, sí, picarilla
Porque si te pillan
Pondrán tu cabeza en la guillotina [own trans.]

His opera *Fidelio* takes place in a jail near the Spanish city of Seville.

When Goya first began painting, he would copy Baroque scenes at José Luzán's academy, before later following Mengs's Neoclassical style, emphasizing the silhouettes of his figures. Only after that would he pioneer a style of his own, bringing together the best elements of the Spanish School, that had been partly forgotten with the emergence of French and Italian works. He is known as Spain's first Romantic painter.

Romanticism began in Germany and Britain in the mid-eighteenth century, and Goya was the first Spaniard to combine artistic realism with popular sentiment, violence, madness, and monstrosity in a unique presentation of imagination and fantasy. He used swift, loose, sketchy brush-strokes to depict the colours of nature and the contrasts of light and shade. Some of his *Costumbrista* or genre paintings — like those portraying the bandit ***Maragato*** — were serialized, giving a sense of movement which anticipates photography and film.

In similarly pioneering fashion, Beethoven introduced the sentiment and emotion of Romanticism in his work, with more chromatic notes, longer compositions and larger orchestras, sonatas for voice and piano based on folk tunes and rural scenes and modifying the number and arrangement of movements.

In 1792, Goya suffered hearing loss as a result of an illness that manifested in Seville. After a slow and painful recovery in Cádiz, he returned to Madrid in a state of profound and irreversible deafness which led him to resign from his responsibilities at the Royal Tapestry Factory and as Director of Painting at the San Fernando Royal Academy in a letter that read as follows:

Your Lordship. I am informing Your Worship that yesterday evening I attended the meeting on principles, and despite my efforts and desire to be useful, I have now lost hope of serving any purpose, as I was unable to hear anything that was said to me and was the cause of some amusement among the boys: I must apologize but Your Worship must take the appropriate decision in consequence.[32]

Most medical research conducted to date agrees on the diagnosis of saturnism, caused by the lead used as a basic element to prepare white paint. Lead poisoning was common at the time and known as "painter's colic" leading not only to colic, but to limb paralysis and temporary blindness and deafness, which in Goya's case proved permanent.

Goya's remains in the Royal Chapel of Saint Anthony of La Florida in Madrid have not yet been examined. The remains do not include his head as this appears to have been removed before burial by a group of physicians who were also phrenology enthusiasts and used it in gruesome experiments.

Lead poisoning is also said to lead to fits of rage, bad temper, and depression. Anger itself has physical effects, including increased blood pressure, heart rate and adrenalin levels, which can lead to violence and aggression in response to a perceived threat or damage.

One such fit of rage has been documented, namely Goya's attempt to attack the Duke of Wellington for criticizing one of the portraits Goya painted of him. A similar outburst is recorded for Beethoven, who reacted violently to the news that Napoleon had been crowned emperor, striking out and tearing up the

---

[32] Muy Señor mío. Participo a Vm. que asistí anoche a la sala de principios: y por más esfuerzos que mis deseos de ser útil perdí la esperanza por ahora de poder servir; por no oír nada de lo que me decían, y ser causa de la diversión de los muchachos: Yo lo siento pero es preciso que Vm. tome la decisión que corresponda

dedication to him that he had intended to include with the score of his *Symphony No. 3, "Heroic."*

It was also in 1792, before he was 30, that Beethoven began to lose his own sense of hearing, shortly after leaving Bonn to take lessons from Joseph Haydn in Vienna. By 1823, he was completely deaf. Overcoming the extreme difficulty that deafness imposes on a musician, he nevertheless managed to continue composing until the end of his days. At the premiere of Symphony No. 9, Beethoven was conducting with his back to the audience, which he could therefore neither see nor hear. He had to be physically turned around to watch their rapturous applause. The symphony's score was added to UNESCO's Memory of the World Programme.

In 2000, a tuft of Beethoven's hair, taken on the day after his death, was analysed by the Pfeiffer Research Center in Naperville, Illinois, USA, which concluded that he too had suffered from lead poisoning, leading to deafness, and recording saturnism as the cause of death. Another analysis on a part of the skull extracted from the corpse in 1863 was conducted in 2005 at the Argonne National Laboratory in Chicago, the DNA of which was confirmed. In both cases, the lead concentration of the remains examined was a hundred times higher than normal. Possible causes include the lead acetate used to sweeten wine, the lead alloy used in goblets and the high concentration of lead in drinking water from a tributary of the Danube that passed close to the composer's house

Both men attended meetings which shared the liberal ideas of Enlightenment intellectuals, nobility and clergy who supported the freedom they believed the French Revolution would bring. But in their political thought, they gave priority to human freedom and always rejected any form of tyranny.

As free, independent individuals, they opposed authoritarian government action of any kind, whether police repression under the Austrian emperor after Napoleon's defeat, in the case of Beethoven, or the absolutist, inquisitorial methods adopted by Ferdinand VII on his return from France, which Goya openly criticized and which ultimately resulted in his exile to Bordeaux, where he died.

In 1813, Beethoven composed *Wellington's Victory* or *Battle of Vitoria* to celebrate the defeat which the combined British, Spanish and Portuguese army inflicted on Napoleon's troops in Vitoria.

Protecting and caring for members of their family was important to both men. Goya took financial responsibility for his parents and the wellbeing of his brothers and sisters and was attentive to his sick wife. He showed great affection for his only surviving son Javier and particularly for his grandson Mariano, who was with him when he died in Bordeaux.

Beethoven died single but adopted his nephew Karl with whom he had a fraught relationship and who rebelled against him on many occasions, but nevertheless accompanied the composer in his final days.

Numerous love affairs have been attributed to both men: to Goya, the dalliances of his youth, and with *majas*, aristocrats and actresses, both single and married; and to Beethoven with young pupils like Josephine Brunsvik, who became Countess Deym, as well as with married women. Such affairs were not made public, owing partly to the strict moral codes of their day.

Both men were said to have suffered from unrequited love, in Goya's case, allegedly for the Duchess of Alba, and in Beethoven's, his "Immortal Beloved." As we have seen, however, Goya's relationship with the Duchess of Alba, which lasted many years, was in fact closer to kinship and affection.

Beethoven and Goya were both pioneers in their fields. The impressionistic style was anticipated by Goya's micro-shades which spring from his brush like tiny drops, flooding the canvas with a striking range of colour, as in ***The Milkmaid of Bordeaux***. The fast drawing, brilliant colours and intensity of the moment captured in the executions of ***The Third of May 1808*** inspired the Impressionist Manet to paint *The Execution of Emperor Maximilian.*

Indeed, Goya's influence can be seen in many major works of modern art, including Dalí, Picasso's *Bulls* or Munch's *Scream*. The mural ***Dog*** in the Quinta del Sordo villa is an early representation of abstract art, using ochre in a variety of intensities and distinct brush strokes to suggest the animal's infinite surroundings and convey a sense of stifling powerlessness and absence of freedom.

As with the etchings of his youth, where he followed Tiepolo, Goya was probably one of the first artists to use the lithograph — initially invented to reproduce written words and music — as it appears in the 1825 series ***The Bulls of Bordeaux***, where he fine-tuned the technique on stones perfectly prepared by the printer Gaulon.

For his part, Beethoven's harmonic changes and progressions influenced jazz, while the underlying bass rhythms of his sonatas where different scales combine and volume, notes, and timbre contrast for emphasis, can be considered to anticipate rock music.

Goya's religious sentiment was both simple and profound. In a letter of 1780, he tells his friend Martín Zapater that, for the house he was looking for in Zaragoza while painting the ***Regina Martyrum*** dome, "I have no need of much furniture, just a print of Our Lady of the Pillar, a table, five chairs, a frying pan, a wineskin, a *tiple,*[33] a spit and an oil lamp, everything else is surplus to requirements." In another of his letters, he declares his faith and hope of attaining Glory.

---

[33] A chordophone of the guitar family

Goya's religious faith is also reflected in paintings with an aura of mystique like the ***Last Communion of Saint Joseph Calasanz*** *(Última comunión de San José de Calasanz)* where God the Father descends from heaven in a beam of light as God the Spirit. The priest becomes a human instrument of the transubstantiation of God the Son in the bread as he places the host delicately in the mouth of the saint who, on the verge of death, receives it with an expression of piety and hope on his pale face. He is accompanied by the clerics of the Piarist schools and the innocent children they took in. Goya painted himself as a member of the order to the right of the saint and his grandson Mariano among the boys with him. Victor Hugo, who was a pupil at the school when his father was French ambassador in Madrid, is also represented.

In his final years in Bordeaux, by this time close to death, Goya put aside his earlier anticlerical drawings and depicted religious themes where kind-hearted clergy help the poor and helpless. An example is the spiritual concentration of the cleric in ***Prayer*** *(Reza)* and ***Monks in Procession*** *(Frailes en procession)*, the humility of ***Friar*** (Fraile) and ***Penitent Monk*** (*Monje en penitencia)* or the holy death of ***The Hermit*** (*El Ermitaño*).

In his last will and testament, Goya expressly requested for his shroud the friar's habit of Saint Francis of Paola, the saint after whom he was named, and thus he was buried in the Catholic cemetery of La Chartreuse in Bordeaux, where he is now celebrated with a monument, as his mortal remains were later transferred to Spain.

For his part, Beethoven's religious faith is perhaps best expressed in his Ninth Symphony, which sends up a prayer that God be found above the universe's canopy of stars, through human love, implicit in the deeply beautiful adagio of its third movement and explicit in the vibrant "Ode to Joy" of the fourth, which is now the official anthem of the European Union. Beethoven sought God in difficult moments of his life and received Holy Communion and last rites before his death and subsequent burial in the Catholic cemetery of Vienna.

Finally, both men's fame lives on in cultural and artistic events that continue to take place all over the world. In April 2020, a magnificent exhibition in the Bundeskunsthalle in Bonn commemorated the 250th anniversary of Beethoven's birth, where parallels were drawn with Goya's life, and which included twenty prints from the series ***The Disasters of War*** in memory of the Peninsular War which Beethoven also recalled in the orchestral work mentioned based on *The Battle of Vitoria,* where the army commanded by Arthur Wellesley, the future Duke of Wellington, defeated Napoleon, putting an end to the armed conflict.

Epilogue

Just as roots nourish the aerial part of the plant with organic elements and minerals transported by water from the soil, giving it life, so the experiences of infancy and youth help mould our thinking and the spirit that governs our lives in adulthood.

For Francisco de Goya y Lucientes, the artistic origins of his father's side of the family — stone masons and gilders who crafted religious and civil works — had a bearing on his vocation as a painter. From the farmers on his mother's side, with whom he lived for the first thirteen years of his life, he learned the value of tireless hard work in the fields and knew that yields were subject to the vagaries of the weather.

He experienced an intense and protective relationship with his parents and grandparents and learned a respect for his elders that would have an ongoing influence on his life when he became the source of financial support, and career sponsor, for his parents, brothers, and sister. When he married, he took care of his wife, son, and grandson, and when he was widowed, he took in his final companion and her daughter.

In Fuendetodos, he enjoyed the life of freedom and security of a country boy who could roam the streets and fields in the company of his childhood playmates, enjoying the landscape, the changing colours of the seasons and rural festivities, all of which would remain firmly engraved on his mind. His grandfather initiated him into the art of hunting, and he would later accompany his uncles on day trips that started in the early hours and took in the plains, pine forests and ravines where they hunted small game. On dark winter nights, when the wind whistled around the hearth where the family gathered, the way to bed was lit by oil lamps which cast gigantic shadows on the walls of the house, instilling a sense of terror that would later emerge in his Black Paintings.

His years in Zaragoza were marked by frenetic social and artistic activity. He attended high-society salons which debated the latest line in liberal and enlightened thought. He took part in *romería* processions and popular picnics where young men and women were initiated into the art of courting, and he was caught up in riots caused by the social and economic hardship into which the city was plunged, aggravated by a prevailing lawlessness and opportunistic criminals.

Books and the theatre provided Goya with the characters, customs and thought that feature in many of his drawings. He had a vast library which covered topics from the clergy and their vices to rogues and prostitution, the Inquisition and decadent nobility, to fables, animals, witches, and goblins. He was an avid spectator of classic dramas and comedies, and enjoyed the farcical sketches of Ramón de la Cruz, inhabited by the popular figures and festive settings which Goya would later depict in his work.

His enthusiasm for bullfighting inspired his brilliant etchings on the subject, depicting its history, the aesthetic expression of the matadors' moves, and the terrible incidents he witnessed at the *corridas*. He produced a self-portrait executing a bullfighting pass with his cape, drew magnificent portraits of bullfighter friends, and mingled with Enlightenment figures who, like him, achieved popularity and fame with hard work and artistic skill.

He was a good friend to his friends and stayed in touch with his earliest schoolmates from Zaragoza, like Martín Zapater with whom his relationship was fraternal and epistolary. In some cases, he became part of the family, as with his kinship with the Bayeu brothers, whose sister he married, and his son's father-in-law Martín Goicoechea whose close friendship lasted into their joint exile in Bordeaux. He visited Infanta María Teresa de Vallabriga and her family in Arenas de San Pedro when they had been banished from court. He accompanied the Duchess of

Alba to Sanlúcar de Barrameda when she was widowed, where he produced magnificent portraits and scenes of her everyday family life.

Music enlivened and enriched many moments in his life. In Fuendetodos, he was moved by the traditional *jotas* where young dancers spun colourful ribbons around them on feast days. In Zaragoza, he would accompany the *seguidilla* and *tirana* dances on his guitar on rowdy nights out in taverns with friends, and he frequented classical music recitals and opera arias whose leading figures — such as his childhood friend Pedro Mocarte and the famous soprano La Tirana — he portrayed.

When he moved to Madrid, Goya's mother gave him a list of names of members of the nobility she recommended he visit. Although there is no record of whether Goya made use of this information, the minor nobility of his ancestors was seared on his memory when he had to buff up his aristocratic credentials and invoke his status as *hidalgo* in order to be hired as court painter. This in turn aided his integration into the royal and upper-class society he would later paint, despite his inferior rank.

He expressed his attitude to religion as sustenance for a simple, humble life, where he claimed to need nothing but a print of Our Lady of the Pillar, a table, five chairs, a frying pan, a wineskin, a tiple, a spit and an oil lamp. He painted many religious themes and saints but had no bones about denouncing the vices of the clergy and the superstitions of the people. For his shroud, he requested the habit of Saint Francis, after whom he was named, and was buried in Bordeaux's Catholic cemetery.

Goya is perhaps the Prado Museum's greatest artist and Spain's universal ambassador, providing an insight into Spanish life in the second half of the eighteenth and the early years of the nineteenth century. It is surprising that, after more than two hundred years of research on the life and work of Goya, with thousands of books, articles, publications, studies, plays, poems, documentaries, films and other forms of artistic expression, that are the work of renowned thinkers, historians, researchers and experts of all nationalities, the director of the Prado Museum, Miguel Falomir, should have argued that "the catalogue has been refined after reflection on earlier attributions to Goya that are currently unsustainable", when presenting Volume II of the new *catalogue raisonné* of Goya's work, published in 2018."

Such "reflection on earlier attributions" led to the removal of ***The Colossus*** *(El coloso)* based on an incorrect technical report which was bitterly contested by Carlos Foradada in his book *Pinturas negras y el coloso*. The administrative procedure was hasty and opaque. Similarly, Julián Vidal (2017), in his book *Goya y el Canal Imperial de Aragón* is of the view that "such an inexplicable delisting was not supported by well-grounded research or a consensus decision, but merely a perlocutionary act issued to the media by the curator M. Mena."

The Museum's anodyne and vapid attribution of this picture to a "Follower of Francisco de Goya" caused considerable embarrassment at the time. As the American Hispanist and Fine Arts Professor of San Fernando and San Carlos Jonathan Brown pointed out (2009), the professional responsibility of an art historian requires that, when removing a canonical painting from the corpus of a great painter, the obligation be met to identify who might have been capable of executing the work.

The Goya print exhibition at the Metropolitan Museum in New York featured ***Seated Giant*** *(Gigante sentado)* as its promotional image and provided an appropriate framework in which to study and resolve the authorship of *The Colossus*. In this respect, the curator Mark McDonald argued that he believed it was indeed by Goya, seeing the two works as related and intertwined, like the same thing at two different moments. In July 2021, the Prado changed the label, which now reads "Attributed to Goya."

In the presentation of the critical catalogue cited above, the director continued as follows:

> We have to update the knowledge that has accrued over the course of almost two centuries, and moreover, paradoxically, explain a large number of the drawings that have barely been studied or explained in the context of the artist's thought. The same is true of his painting.[34]

In this "new context", which seeks to reinterpret the artist's thought, however, Goya has been categorized by some as an anti-bullfighting homosexual, as we saw in Chapters 6 and 8. A simple glance at the opinion of the manservant who accompanied his master to Fuendetodos in 1808 would surely leave us in little doubt as to Goya's preferences: "My master is incorrigible about two things: his fondness for bullfighting and his fondness for the daughters of Eve."

Goya's life and work have been studied in general and in detail on many occasions, highlighting the genius of his prints and the magic of his portraits and landscapes. But recently, unjustified assertions have been made that stem from a prevailing relativism, a desire for visibility or to misrepresent his life for personal convenience or entertainment purposes, producing programmes and documentaries replete with fake news and false opinions. Perhaps it is the price that the great figures of history must pay.

---

[34] Translated from the Spanish catalogue

In 1802, the Spanish poet Gregorio Salas alluded to attacks of precisely this kind in an epigram:

> You surpass nature
> And your fame will be eternal
> If only envy does not kill
> Nature itself[35]

Zaragoza, 12 October, 2021

---

[35] La naturaleza excedes
Y tu fama será eterna,
Si de envidia no la mata /La misma naturaleza.

Bibliography

ABC. El Prado, sobre Goya: "Que los hombres transmitan afectos no implica ninguna sexualidad." Cultura, 11 December 2018.

Andolz, Rafael. *Diccionario aragonés*. Librería General, Zaragoza, 1977.

Águeda, Mercedes y Xavier de Salas. *Cartas a Martín Zapater*. Francisco de Goya, Ediciones Istmo, 2003

Alcalá Flecha, Roberto. *Literatura e ideología en el arte de Goya*. Diputación General de Aragón, 1988

Amón, Rubén. "Goya era taurino y homosexual, ¿también vegano y hipster?" El Confidencial. 29 November 2019.

Amorós, Andrés. "¿Un Goya anti taurino?" ABC Cultural, 8 December 2019.

Anes, Gonzalo. *El antiguo régimen de los Borbones*. Ediciones Alfaguara. Alianza Editorial, Madrid, 1975.

Ansón Navarro, Arturo. *Goya y Aragón*. Caja de Ahorros de la Inmaculada de Aragón, Zaragoza, 1995.

Ansorena, Javier. "El Gigante sentado y el Coloso, dos caras de la misma moneda." ABC Cultural, 9 February 2021.

Antequera, José. "Goya, el animalista anti taurino." Diario 16, 29 December 2019.

Arroyos J. Carlos. "Ordenación de Explotaciones en la Comarca de Sástago." MAP. Iryda Información nº 25, 1978.

Arroyos J. Carlos. *Las tierras roturadas en Aragón*. Gran Enciclopedia Aragonesa UNALI,1981.

Arroyos J. Carlos. *Desarrollo Rural Sostenible en la UE*. Ministerio de Agricultura, Pesca y Alimentación. Mundi-Prensa, 2007.

Arteaga, Almudena.*Alonso de Ceballos*.Ediciones Montalbo, 1997.

Astorga, Antonio. "Interview with Antonio Mingote." ABC, 27 July 2008.

Baeza, José. *Francisco de Goya*. Colección los grandes hombres, 1928.

Bango Torviso, Isidro G. *El Camino de Santiago*. BBVA, Espasa Calpe, 1993.

Blasco Martínez, Rosa María. *Zaragoza en el siglo XVIII*. Librería General, Zaragoza, 1977.

Baticle, Jeannine. *Francisco de Goya*. ABC S.L. Editorial Folio, 2004.

Benlloch, José Luis. "Ahora pretenden que Goya sea anti taurino." Las Provincias, 24 November 2019.

Belchite. *Currículo de la enseñanza en las escuelas de esa época*. Published in Zaragoza. Oficina de Ibáñez, 1803.

Buesa, Domingo J. *'El retrato de la madre de Goya'*. El Periódico de Aragón, November 2021

CAI. *Aragón constante histórica*. Gráficas Estella S.A., 1978.

Canellas López, Ángel (ed.). *Goya y Lucientes, Francisco*. Tomo XI. Ediciones Rialp S.A, Madrid, 1981.

Carazo, Luis. "Beethoven" Cuaderno de Notas, 2019.

Carrasco de Jaime, Daniel José. *De la luz y de las sombras G.O.Y.A.* Editorial Edaf, 2019.

Castán Palomar, Fernando. *Vida de D. Francisco de Goya y Lucientes*. Editorial Juventud S.A., Barcelona, 1994.

Censo de Aranda. *Estado general de la población de España en los años 1768 y 1789*. Madrid,1999.

Centellas Salamero, Ricardo. *De Goya al cambio de siglo (1800-1920)*. Ibercaja, 2002.

Cervantes, Miguel. *Don Quijote de la Mancha*. Biblioteca Clásica, Instituto Cervantes, 1998.

Conde de la Viñaza. *Goya, su tiempo, su vida y sus obras*. Madrid, 1887.

Conde de Toreno. *Histoire du soulévement de la guerre et de la révolution d'Espagne*. Spanish edition BAE, t.LXIV, 1835.

Corral, José Luis. "Genio Universal." ABC, 5 August 2018.

Corral, José Luis. *Historia contada de Aragón*. Librería General S.A, Zaragoza, 2000.

Cultura. "El Prado duda que la carta del pintor Goya a un amigo implique que fuera gay y lo tilda de 'afecto entre hombres'." 20 minutos, 11 December 2018.

Chabrun, Jean François. *Grandes maestros. Goya*. Ediciones Daimon, 1986.

De Asso, Ignacio. *Historia de la Economía política de Aragón*. Francisco Magallón, 1798.

De Azara, José Nicolás. *Obras de D. Antonio Rafael Mengs, primo pintor de Cámara del Rey*, 1780.

De Horna, Antonio. *Obras de Goya: La Tauromaquia, Los Caprichos, Las tragedias, Los Toros de Burdeos y otras litografías. Grabados varios*. Madrid, Ediciones de Arte, 1971.

De Pano y Ruata, Mariano. *Colección. Goya y Aragón*. CAI Zaragoza, 1995.

De Salas, Gregorio. *Epigramas*, 1802.

Del Arco, Ricardo. *Pinturas de Goya en el Oratorio de los Condes de Sobradiel*, 1915.

Diputación Provincial de Zaragoza. *Tierra de Belchite, valle del Huerva y campos de Cariñena*. 2010.

Domínguez, José A. and Olona José L. *Fuendetodos: los paisajes que Goya conoció*. Flora montibérica, 1997.

Donézar Díez de Ulzurrun, Javier M. *Riqueza y propiedad en la Castilla del Antiguo Régimen*. Ministerio de Agricultura, Pesca y Alimentación,1996.

D'Ors, Eugenio. *Goya*. Libertarias, 1996.

D'Olhaberriague, Concha. "De Madrid al cielo." ABC Suplemento Alfa Omega, 13 December 2018.

El románico. *La arquitectura en Europa*. Ediciones Castilla S. A. Madrid, 1963.

El Universal. "Cartas no revelan si Goya era Gay": El Prado. Cultura,11 December 2018.

Exhibition at Palacio de Sástago, Zaragoza. *Goya y sus inicios académicos*. Diputación General de Aragón, 1996.

Exhibition brochure. *La memoria de Goya. Tras los pasos de Goya en Zaragoza*. Museo Provincial de Zaragoza, March 2008.

Exhibition brochure. *La memoria de Goya*. Museo Provincial de Zaragoza, March 2008.

Exhibition brochure Goya. *Sus raíces aragonesas* 1746-1775. Museo Goya. Colección Ibercaja. Exhibition in Zaragoza, 26 February to 28 June 2015.

Exhibition *"Goya: The portraits"*, *"Goya, un espectáculo de carne y hueso."* Documentary on the exhibition at the National Gallery in London, shown in cinemas by Documentalia, 2015.

Ezpeleta Carmen Aguilar. *Senderos turísticos de Aragón. Fuendetodos-La Puebla de Albortón. Folklore y antropología de la cuenca turolense de Utrillas-Montalbán*, 1991.

Fatas, Guillermo. "Goya, Beethoven y Napoleón." Heraldo de Aragón, 13 December 2020.

Fernández Ardavín. *De Capa y espada*, 1914.

Fernández Moratín, N. *Memorias sobre los medios de fomentar sólidamente la agricultura en un país, sin detrimento de la cría de ganados, y el modo de remover los obstáculos que puedan impedirla.* Memorias de la Sociedad Económica de Madrid, 1780.

Fernández Moratín, Leandro. *Quema de brujas en Logroño.* La Máscara, 1999.

Fuendeverde. Field notebook. level 1 & 2. *Senderos y caminos de Fuendetodos*. 2019.

Fondation Beyeler. Riehen, Basel.*Goya exhibition catalogue,* 10 October 2021 to 23 January 2022.

Fundación Botín and Museo Nacional del Prado *Catalogue raisonné. Volume II (1771-1792). Francisco de Goya. Dibujos.* Fundación Botín and Museo Nacional del Prado, 2018.

Fundación Goya en Aragón: On-line catalogue, 2021.

Gállego, Julián. *Goya y la caza*. Ediciones el Viso. Madrid, 1985.

Garcia, Ángeles. "Goya, ¿pionero del movimiento anti taurino?" El País, 26 April 2016.

García, Juan Cristóbal. "El Museo del Prado insiste en que Goya era anti taurino, ¿qué hay de cierto?" Aplausos, 29 November 2019.

García Calero, Jesús. "El extraño caso del Prado y El Coloso." ABC, 2 April 2013.

García Calero, Jesús. Cuando "Goya fue rechazado por la Academia." ABC Cultural, 6 February 2021.

García Calero, Jesús. "El Coloso gana el combate."ABC Cultura, 12 July 2021.

García Julián, Javier. *Goya. Cómo se hizo gran pintor.* Tipografía La Academia, Zaragoza, 1923.

García, Fernando. "Goya, sus dibujos y su 'amigo amoroso." La Vanguardia. 6 December 2018.

García, Mariano "El año Goya empieza este lunes en Fuendetodos y ofrecerá 12 exposiciones." Heraldo de Aragón, 6 February 2021.

Gassier, Pierre and Juliet Wilson. *Vida y obra de Francisco de Goya.* Editorial Juventud, Barcelona, 1974.

Gaya Nuño, Juan Antonio. "Las pinturas mitológicas de Goya." Goya revista de arte nº 100, Madrid, 1971.

Glendinning, Nigel. *La década de los Caprichos. Goya. Retratos 1792-1804*, Real Academia de Bellas Artes de San Fernando, 1992.

Gómez de la Serna, Ramón. *Goya*. Espasa Calpe, 1958.

"Goya y su contexto." Institución Fernando El Católico. Seminar, 2011.

Gran Enciclopedia Aragonesa. *Tierras roturadas*. Unión Aragonesa del Libro. Unali S.L., 1982.

Guía turística de Aragón. PRAMES, 2003.

Helmut, C. Jacobs. *El sueño de la razón. El capricho 43 de Goya en el arte visual, la literatura y la música*. Editorial Iberoamericana, Madrid, 2011.

Helmut, C. Jacobs. *Goya en la poesía*. Institución Fernando El Católico, 2017.

Heraldo de Aragón. Documentary: "Así somos", 2015.

Herbert Henkins. *Francisco de Goya. Its work and personality*. Hugh Stokes, 1913.

Heritage. "La música de Madrid en los tiempos de Goya." Folleto del Concierto del Cuarteto Quiroga en el Museo del Prado el 1 febrero 2020.

Manuel Hernáiz, José. *Cuaderno italiano*. Electa, 1996.

Jarnés, Benjamín. *Lecciones de Goya*. Institución Fernando El Católico, 1988.

Junta del Centenario de Goya. *Catorce visiones en torno a Goya.* Publicaciones, Gobierno de Aragón,1996.

Lacarra, José María. *Aragón en el pasado.* Colección Austral, Espasa Calpe, Madrid, 1977.

López González, Juan-Jaime. *La Ciudad. de Zaragoza a finales de siglo XVIII.* Institución Fernando El Católico, 1977.

López Rey, J. *Goya y su mundo alrededor.* Editorial Sudamericana, Buenos Aires, 1947.

Lorenci, Miguel. "Las cartas de Goya a Zapater no permiten afirmar ni negar que fuera homosexual." Heraldo de Aragón, 12 December 2018.

Losada, Basilio. *Goya.* Verón Editor,1970.

Madoz, Pascual. *Diccionario Geográfico-Estadístico-Histórico de España*, Madrid, 1847.

Marcén, Daniel. "Los trigos del secano aragonés." Ecomonegros 03.

Marcial, Marco Valerio. *Epigramas.* Milán, Archivo del Gobierno da Aragón, 1490.

Martín Zorraquino, María Antonia y Estrella Montolío Durán. (coords). *Los marcadores del discurso. Teoría y análisis.* Arco / Libros, Madrid, 1998.

Matheron, Laurent. *Goya.* Biblioteca Universal, Madrid, 1890.

Matilla and Mena. *Goya. Drawings. Only my strength of will remains.* Museo del Prado. Exhibition. 2019-2020.

Mayer A.L. *Francisco de Goya.* Barcelona, 1925.

Ministerio de Agricultura. *Mapa de cultivos y aprovechamientos.* Madrid, 2010.

Multiple authors. *Goya.* Muy arte. Edición coleccionista. La razón de la pintura. October 2021

Ona González, José Luis and Cinta Yago, Jaime. (coords). *Comarca Campo de Belchite.* Colección Territorio 35. Gobierno de Aragón, 2010.

Onieva, Antonio J. *Goya*. Editorial Offo, Madrid, 1973.

Ortega y Gasset, José. *Goya*. Revista de Occidente. Madrid, 1962.

Palacios Remondo, Félix. *Goya o Bayeu. Historia oculta de un boceto del siglo XVIII. El borroncico de Goya*. Fundación Goya en Aragón. Real Academia de Nobles y Bellas Artes de San Luis. 2014

Pardo Porto, Bruno. "Nueva polémica por el supuesto carácter antitaurino de Goya." ABC. 23 November 2019.

Perdomo Carmona, Marialys. *Contribución al estudio de los marcadores discursivos en un corpus del español actual de Cuba*. Doctoral thesis, Universidad de Zaragoza, 2020.

Pérez Gracia, César. "La maja del Jiloca en Budapest y Dublín." Heraldo de Aragón, 2011.

Pérez Trullen, José María. *La psicopatología de Goya y su influencia en su creatividad artística*. Doctoral thesis, 2014.

Piaget Jean. *Psicología del niño*. Ediciones Morata, 2015.

Pool Novelo, Luciano. "Las Pausas de la Tierra", Revista Ecofrontera, pp.35. Ecosur.Mex, 2015.

Quant, Roger. "Notas sobre la psicología evolutiva", 2016.

Rodríguez-Moñino, Antonio. *Goya y Gallardo. Noticias sobre su amistad. De Amadís a Goya*. Castalia, Madrid, 1959.

Rodriguez Pablo, L. "La abuela de Goya no era española." El País Cultural. 20 June 2021

Rodríguez Sánchez de León, Mª José. *La crítica en el teatro barroco español (siglosXVII-XIX)*. Ediciones Almar, Salamanca, 2000.

Romero Tobar, Leonardo. *Goya en las literaturas*. Marcial Pons Historia S.A., Madrid, 2016.

Rotellar Mata, Manuel. *Gran Enciclopedia Aragonesa. Goya*. 1981.

Ruiz Lasala, Inocencio. *Goya visto por un librero zaragozano*. Diputación General de Aragón, 1989.

Sambricio, Valentín. *Tapices de Goya*. Patrimonio Nacional, 1946.

Sánchez-Grande, Goya." El Prado y la falacia de Goya anti taurino." El Mundo. 21 November 2019.

Sánchez Salazar, Felipa. *Extensión de cultivos en España en el siglo XVIII*. Ministerio de Agricultura, Pesca y Alimentación, 1988.

Sánchez Cantón, Francisco y Bermejo, Cándido. *Vida y Obras de Goya*. Institución Fernando El Católico, 1951.

Sánchez Cantón, Francisco. *Los niños en las obras de Goya. Goya: cinco estudios*. Institución Fernando El Católico, p 67-88, 1978.

Sánchez Grande, Gloria. "El Prado y la falacia de Goya anti taurino." El Mundo, 21 November 2019.

Sánchez-Lassa, Ana. "El origen vasco de Goya." Lecture at Zerain Casa de la Cultura, November 2018.

Sánchez, Imanol "Las pruebas que constatan que Goya fue aficionado a la tauromaquia", 29 October 2019.

Sánchez Salazar Felipe. *Extensión de cultivos en España en el siglo XVIII*. Ministerio de Agricultura, Pesca y Alimentación, 1988.

Sanchis Sinisterra, José: *Monsieur Goya. Una indagación*. Play performed at Fernán Gómez Theatre, Madrid in Sept-Nov. 2019

Sarasúa García, Carmen. *El nivel de vida en la España rural del siglo XIX*. Universidad de Alicante, 2002.

Solanilla, José Luis. "Fuendetodos será sede de la muestra ¿Goya en un Hospital?" Heraldo de Aragón, 8 August 2020.

Tausiet, María. *Los posesos de Tosos*. Instituto Aragonés de Antropología, 1998

Tausiet, María. *Los posesos de Tosos (1812-1814). Brujería y justicia popular en tiempos de revolución*. Editoriales Cometa S. A., Zaragoza, 2002.

Thomas, Hugh: *Goya. El tres de mayo de 1808*. Ediciones Grijalbo, Barcelona, 1979.

Tomlinson, Janis A. "Goya de paseo por Madrid. Retrato del artista en su juventud." El País. Cultura, 19 November 2014.

Tomlinson, Janis A. *A Portrait of the Artist*. Princeton University Press, 2020.

Torralba Soriano, Federico. "Notas sobre algunas obras de la juventud de Goya en Aragón." Revista de Arte Goya. Nº 100. Madrid, 1971.

Torralba Soriano, Federico. *El entorno familiar de Goya*. Ibercaja, 1990.

Tsanis, Magdalena. "El Prado defiende la heterosexualidad. de Goya: Transmitir afectos no implica adscripción a una sexualidad." El Español, 11 December 2018.

TV Aragón. *Desmontando a Goya*, documentary, 2018.

Uribarri, Fátima. "Goya dibujando a Velázquez." ABC. XL semanal, 5 January 2020.

Umschau Verlag. *La arquitectura en Europa. El románico.* Frankfurt, 1959.

Ventura Remacha, Benjamín. *El regreso a Zaragoza de D. Francisco el de los Toros.* Diputación de Zaragoza, 1991.

Vidal, Julián. *Goya y el Canal Imperial de Aragón.* Diputación Provincial de Zaragoza. Institución Fernando El Católico, 2017.

Videgaín, José. *Diccionario de aragonés para foranos.* Mira Editores S. A., Zaragoza, 2015.

Video de la Diputación Provincial de Zaragoza. *Goya y Fuendetodos.* Arte y Cultura. 2013.

Zapater y Gómez, Francisco. Goya. *La memoria de Goya. Tras los pasos de Goya en Zaragoza.* Fundación Goya en Aragón, 2008.

Zapater y Gómez, Francisco. *Noticias biográficas.* Imprenta de la Perseverancia, Zaragoza,1868.

Ingram Content Group UK Ltd.
Milton Keynes UK
UKHW051342250623
423907UK00012B/113